Corporate Citizenship

THE ROLE OF COMPANIES AS CITIZENS OF THE MODERN WORLD

DAVID LOGAN

Corporate Citizenship

First published in 2018 by

Panoma Press Ltd
48 St Vincent Drive, St Albans, Herts, AL1 5SJ, UK
info@panomapress.com
www.panomapress.com

Book layout by Neil Coe.

Printed on acid-free paper from managed forests.

ISBN 978-1-784521-50-9

Dedication

This book is dedicated to my wife, Gaye Pedlow. She and I met in 1982 as we were just launching out on our individual careers in corporate responsibility work, which has been part of our lives to the present day.

Acknowledgements

As to the ideas I put forward in the book with regard to corporate citizenship, I owe a great debt to Peter E. Haas, the CEO and President of Levi Strauss & Co. during my time working there. He and his brother Walter Hass Jnr, and their wider families, struggled with what it was to be a commercially successful business that acted in the world on decent values. While they created the ethos of the business, others in the San Francisco management team, such as Tom Harris and Bob Dunn, introduced me to many new ideas and practical activities in the world of corporate responsibility.

I initially experienced the company's values and policies working in the Northern European Division of the company. There, the Divisional CEO Robin Dow, plant managers such as Alex MacMillan and Jack McKenna, and their human resources staff including Betty Wallace and Margaret Capie all helped shape my experience and ideas. They, along with trade union shop stewards such as Ella Heddon at the North Shields plant, Community Involvement Teams chairpersons such Betty Dow in Dundee and the many members of these volunteer teams in 10 locations in Europe, did so much to demonstrate in practice what a company could do for society, when it accepted a responsibility to be a good citizen.

Working as a consultant after leaving Levi's, I benefitted greatly from the interaction with colleagues such as Mike Tuffrey, Amanda Jordan, Peter Truesdale, Andrew Wilson, Helen Rushton, Peter Hughes and Karin Laljani. We worked together as a team and their contributions to our work in developing the idea of Corporate Citizenship cannot go unmentioned. There are many other members of our staff team who have also helped shape my thinking.

As did the many corporate members of London Benchmarking Group (LBG), with which we co-created a modern system for managing corporate community relations. That work we did in the 1990s rapidly expanded beyond the corporate community interface, often at the behest of the many clients who trusted us with their problems and worked collaboratively with us to address them.

Working with various clients enabled us to do so much to develop the wider corporate responsibility and sustainability agenda. We were able to work on some of the most demanding economic, social and environmental challenges for business. Chief among them are Charlotte Grezo formerly at Vodafone, Mandy Cormack formerly at Unilever, Neil Makin formerly at Cadbury, Peter Heng formerly at Golden Agri in Singapore and Kathy Pickus at Abbott. Each in turn gave me the opportunity to travel the world and work on addressing some of the most urgent and intractable problems companies face today. Their insight and council were invaluable.

While this book is very much based on my practical experience in business life, colleagues in the academic world have been similarly helpful. A special acknowledgement is due to Professor David Grayson of Cranfield University who is an accomplished practitioner and writer in the field of corporate responsibility. He did more than anyone to encourage me to write this book, commenting on early drafts. Thanks are also due to Professor Jennifer Griffin, who taught at George Washington University in Washington DC, and is now at Loyola University in Chicago. She, Mike Tennent at Imperial College London, and David Greyson have each involved me in their teaching work with students to our mutual benefit.

Last, a special thanks is due to Mindy Gibbins-Klein and her team at Panoma Press for the help and support they have given in getting this book written and published.

Preface

This book is based on a lecture I give to young people joining our company, Corporate Citizenship. I set out to give them a context for the work we do. I also set out to challenge some of the ideas about business and its relationship with society, which they might well have acquired at university or from wider society. When I have finished, several of them have said: "You should write a book." So I have.

The book is a longer, expanded version of that lecture, but it has a similar goal. I want to explain why, at this particular time in history, the idea of corporate citizenship has a particular relevance for global society. It is my answer to the great question of my young life, which was: "What is the future of capitalism?" When I was in my twenties in the late 1960s and early 1970s, we thought capitalism was dying and that socialism was becoming the global pattern of social organisation. We never thought about corporate responsibility as an issue because we thought we were not going to have corporations of any great size or significance.

Consequently, this book is not just an argument for, and justification of, the idea of corporate citizenship, it is the story of my intellectual and emotional journey over the past 50 years. One that has led me to the view that business activity is a normal and natural part of human society. As a result, the answer to my question about the future of capitalism today is not to try and eliminate it, as communists and socialists have done in the past, but to work to make it a humane and responsible part of the social whole.

This change of view has come about due to practical work experience as I moved from working for the government as a teacher, then with the British Trades Union Congress as a researcher, and three years in the voluntary sector, where I worked for a profitable community-owned business, the Jubilee Hall in Covent Garden. In 1980 I joined the Community Affairs department of Levi Strauss & Co., working first in Europe then in company headquarters in San Francisco. With that move I changed sides and joined American capitalism, and I got to see it working from the inside.

Thus there is a strong element of memoir in this book. It is very much based on my experience, which is somewhat unusual, but also still limited. For example, I worked in the highly creative world of California for about eight years because when I left Levi's I set up my corporate responsibility consulting business there. However, during this time, I remained firmly in the old economy. I worked for a jeans company, and my first corporate client as a consultant was the Los Angeles-based oil company ARCO. While I did ultimately work in Silicon Valley as a consultant for businesses like 3Com and Sun Microsystems, I was not part of the digital revolution being developed there, and this lack of experience may well show through in the book, particularly as I think about business in the future.

However, the last 20 years or so of my career have been very international and I have had the opportunity to work with a wide range of businesses in oil, mining, Fast-Moving Consumer Goods, mobile phones and banks. I have also worked in countries as diverse as India, China, Peru, Mexico, Turkey, Poland, Ghana, Kenya, Pakistan, Bangladesh, Indonesia and more. These countries and their businesses are still concerned with the impact of firms in the old economy. In fact many of these countries have been living through an economic and social restructuring similar to that we lived through in Britain during the 1980s, and many of the lessons learned in Margaret Thatcher's Britain have had useful applications in other countries.

Another limitation on my experience has been my detailed exposure to environmental issues. When I worked for the Social Responsibility and Ethics Committee at Levi's in the 1980s, we did not focus on them to anything like the degree the company now does. In was only in the late 1970s and into the 1980s that we began to get the large-scale data sets about the impact of CFCs and the potential for global warming. From my trade union days, my focus has been on social and economic issues and they were very much to the fore in a garment company like Levi's. However, over the past 30 years or so we have begun to see that capitalism can be far more inclusive and beneficial than the Marxists ever thought, but that it probably cannot pay the environmental price of its success.

Nevertheless, having worked on deforestation and biodiversity with Golden Agri in Indonesia, I am convinced that the argument I make here has a broad relevance and value in respect of how companies, as the agents of the market, should behave, irrespective of their size or the industry they are in, or whether it is economic, social or environmental issues that we are dealing with.

This book is set out in two halves. The first is my view of the broad sweep of history and how companies have fitted into society in the past and how we should view their role today. It may well be a controversial view for some. It moves rapidly over a lot of profound social, economic and environmental issues in order to make the case for a new approach to corporate citizenship. It sets a broad context for the discussion of corporate citizenship today. The second part of the book sets out an approach, based on my experience, as to how companies should go about defining and managing their role in society. A discussion of both the context and the practical issues of managing good citizenship seems to be necessary to keep this debate moving forward.

This is not an academic book, it is a series of reflections by a practitioner responding to the great political, social and economic changes that have been experienced over a lifetime. Consequently, I have only sought to give references for the big ideas and trends that seem relevant. I have not referenced all the detail of the argument. It is to be hoped that the references give support to the argument and will prompt readers to read more widely about this multidisciplinary topic. Lastly, many of the examples I use to illustrate points are possibly not the most up to date or even the best, but they tend to be ones I know from having worked on the issue.

I hope this book is a useful contribution to the debate about the role of business in society, and that young people thinking about these issues can see where we have come from over the past 40 years or so. I hope also to have identified the sorts of issues companies and others need to take into account in shaping the future of the global economy and the life of humanity as a whole. Private companies are back as key players in shaping human society, and I hope the young people who inspired this book get some useful ideas about the role companies can play in their future.

Contents

PART 1:

THE HISTORICAL AND CULTURAL CONTEXT

Introduction

If you want to discuss the role of business in society, it is important to say something about society itself, and the first section of this book sets a historical and social context for that discussion. This book touches on a wide range of political, economic, religious and cultural issues but deliberately avoids looking at companies and business through the usual left versus right political lens. Neither does it discuss the theory of the free market 'capitalist' system of which companies are a part.

Capitalism is contentious and that will not change. There are many books about free market capitalism, but this one looks at society somewhat differently. It accepts that we live in a 'capitalist' society and that companies are the agents of the market system, so need to identify their role in shaping society for good and ill. It asks the question: what is the role of a company in our modern global society and can companies individually, and in partnership with others, act to promote the common good? This book is arguing that 'corporate citizenship' is an important part of the answer to that question.

Just as society is composed of individuals, families and other social groupings, the market economy is composed of individual companies, large and small, linked together in many different ways. Companies, like individual citizens, have rights and responsibilities in society and are 'corporate' citizens of society. Their behaviour, like that of individuals and families, makes up the character of the social whole. Just as we need to change the attitudes and behaviours of ordinary citizens to promote major aspects of social progress, we need to do the same with companies.

Many will argue that this can only be done through changing laws and compelling companies to behave in a certain way. There will always be a case for legislation to change behaviour, but this book explores how companies, like individuals, can change themselves. It is focused on the company's relations with society and how their behaviour as a business can shape the future for humanity's common good.

The first section of the book tries to set a context to that discussion, to see companies and their behaviour as part of a mix of organisations that human beings have created over time to address their needs, wants and aspirations. The history of the role of private firms is important to understanding their place in society today and speaks to some of the key issues they will need to face in the future.

Private companies are nothing new. They have had a profound impact on shaping human culture, in particular meeting humanity's material needs and wants, since the beginning of recorded history. Records that show the world's first multinationals were trading across Mesopotamia and the Middle East in 2000 BC, while the Phoenicians, Greeks, Romans, the Muslim world, India, China and medieval Europe have all had free market enterprises as part of their social mix of institutions. They have been a major force for economic, social, political and cultural development worldwide, often as a key driver of technical innovation and cross-cultural exchange.

Trading and manufacturing activities of companies and entrepreneurs have made a significant contribution to the development of our global society over the past 400 years, in particular, those new products and services that have been so influential in the creation of the modern world. In Europe in the 17th, 18th and 19th centuries, companies such as the Dutch East India Company (VOC) in the Netherlands, and the British East India Company, were central to developing global trading routes, and bringing a vast number of new products to European and Asian markets. Indonesia, India and other countries were also conquered as part of European colonial expansion, and were often led by private companies seeking new markets, to control raw materials or occasionally to find new sources of labour for the production of raw materials, as in the case of the Atlantic slave trade.

During the Industrial Revolution in Europe, entrepreneurs and companies built factories and mines that saw their workers, including children, working and living in appalling conditions. While a few business owners, such as textile manufacturer Robert Owen,[1] sought to behave well towards his workers by providing extensive social provision in a 'company town', most did not, and the free market *laissez-faire* capitalism on which companies depended fell into radical disrepute.

There were many who opposed the excesses of the free market system, but Karl Marx, in his great work *Das Kapital* [2], best articulated the response of the dispossessed around the world to the capitalist system. In the

Communist Manifesto,[3] published in 1848, he and Friedrich Engels argued for a proletarian revolution to create a new system of society with a rationally planned economy and far greater economic and social equality. The central demand of the communists was the abolition of all forms of private enterprise and large swathes of the globe took up Marx's call. After the Russian Revolution of 1917 until the fall of the Berlin Wall in 1989, the dominant intellectual and political ethos of the time was pro-communist and socialist. Hundreds of millions of people in countries such as Russia and China were living in societies where the existence of private companies was strictly forbidden and all enterprises were owned by the state.

Others, in developing countries such as India, lived under socialist governments determined to overthrow the colonial exploitation of the past and to take many businesses into public control, while controlling in detail the activities of the remaining private companies. Even in Europe, socialist countries such as Sweden permitted the existence of private firms, but kept them firmly under control, while the post-war British government nationalised many private firms that were seen to be the 'commanding heights' of the economy.

North Korea is one of the few countries still on this path of promoting total state control of the economy, and indeed, everyday life in general. It still uses brute force to suppress any form of private economic activity. While socialists around the world strove to reduce the role of the private sector and grow the role of the state, there were many conservative politicians who went along with the post-war consensus of expanding the power of the state and diminishing the role of private enterprise. Following the Second World War, the pendulum had swung against private enterprise, its day was thought to be over, and it was pushed to the margins of many societies, apart from a few countries such as the USA. There, the Federal Government has never had a socialist agenda, perhaps with the exception of the New Deal years, and private companies dominated economic life.

This pattern of a rise, then decline, of private enterprise can be seen repeating throughout history and is the background to Part 1 of this book. In the past 40 years, we have lived through a remarkable period of history when a massive effort, backed by extreme force on occasion, has been made to eliminate private firms, and it has failed. Today private companies are again holding a leading position in the economic, social and environmental development of the world, and it is in this context that a discussion of corporate citizenship has become important.

The change that brought back business as an important influence in global society came about in the West with the election of Prime Minister Margaret Thatcher in 1979 in the UK, and President Reagan who took office in the USA in 1981. They both set out to reverse the trend of history and, among other things, cut taxes. Mrs Thatcher in particular returned a whole raft of businesses from state control back to the private sector. Once they became independent for-profit entities, these new private companies had to define, articulate, and justify their role in society as corporate citizens, just as other private companies had done over the years. In the East, Deng Xiaoping was elected as the paramount leader of the Chinese People's Republic in 1978, and he went on to launch the Four Modernisations, which ultimately led to the creation of a vast number of new private firms in China today.

The first part of the book examines some of the social and political questions about free enterprise and the role of private firms, in society. If we are no longer trying to get rid of private firms, but promoting their development, can we also make them better citizens? Can we help them to be effective partners in economic, social and environmental progress? Acknowledging that at this point in history, after the fall of the Berlin Wall in 1989, and the collapse of the communist project, we seem to have little choice. Companies are the agents of the new global market and drive its development. They have many rights in doing so, but what of their responsibilities to society? The first part of this book argues that companies should recognise those responsibilities, accept them in full, and exercise them in partnership with others.

Those others are the two other formal sectors of society: government and the non-profit sector. Another effect of the scaling back of government's role in society has been the rise of the non-profit sector, which is playing a vital role in shaping the world's future – but it cannot do it alone. It needs to be able to work with both government and private firms if society as a whole is to benefit from these three formal sectors, each of which represent something distinctive in terms of human creativity and experience. Non-profits are important in changing the moral climate of society but if, like the young people in my office, you want to effect change at scale, then you must work with government and the resurgent private sector.

Getting these sectors to work together will not be easy as there are many barriers to mutual understanding between the three formal sectors. They have different roles in society, different goals, and effectively speak different languages. There are also barely articulated psychological inhibitions, which make it difficult for a society to bring the three together for constructive dialogue and action. However, it seems that today we have no choice but to try, and the corporate sector has probably got the most to do to adapt to these new social and political circumstances, which are increasingly global in character.

The first part of the book has a distinct worldview that has taken me, an ex-Trades Union Congress officer, half a lifetime to form. I have had to change not only how I think about business, but how I feel about it too. I had to learn to respect the integrity and ability of those who work in companies and not just view them as 'tools' of capitalism. In order to make progress, I argue that people in all three of the organised sectors need to overcome some entrenched attitudes based on emotional responses to each other and society generally. The problems posed in this part of the book are not just intellectual ones, they are emotional problems too.

I want to help make the best use of the global social system that humanity is almost unconsciously evolving, to move the debate on and push best practice forward for companies in particular. The approach is one of incremental change, but that is how society moves forward. Some will protest that on issues like climate change, we don't have the time for an incremental approach, and who knows? There might indeed be a whole new form of global governance waiting to happen, but I am not banking on it. In the meantime, we have to live our lives and do the best we can with the institutions we have created, including private companies.

Throughout the first part of the book in particular, I have quoted other sources to give support to the argument, not least because corporate responsibility and sustainability is such a multidisciplinary field. It can stretch from religion, values and ethics, global politics and economics, to the detail of tax policy, and environmental science. It is also an intensely practical discipline. A lot of hard and detailed work is necessary to make some very small steps, but that is what makes it rewarding and worthwhile. The second part of the book looks at these issues in more detail.

Meanwhile, the world's companies exist in massive and growing numbers, the largest ones have great power, immense resources and employ millions of highly educated people. We need to work on getting these immensely powerful organisations to step up and play their part as global corporate citizens. Hopefully, an understanding of the historical forces that have brought us to the current situation will add a perspective that will encourage companies to think and act as corporate members of a global society and seek to shape it for the common good.

CHAPTER 1:

Private Companies Are Part of the Development of Human Culture

The World's First Multinationals

When thinking about the role of business in society today, it is important to understand that private companies have been part of human culture since the beginning of recorded history. When I first read an article by Karl Moore and Karl Lewis in the *International Management Review*[4] that argued that the world's first multinationals had been created in Assyria around 2000 BC, I was surprised, indeed, a little shocked. I had always assumed that capitalism and private companies were a distinctly modern phenomenon, arising out of European commercial and industrial innovation in the 17th and 18th centuries. I assumed that private companies were a creation of modern capitalism and the thought that human beings had invented them 4,000 years ago, because they served a useful social purpose, was very challenging.

I was a student in 1968 when Paris erupted with protest against capitalist society and its colonialist wars. Those times represented the high tide mark of communist and socialist thinking and young people around the world felt that capitalism was dying. The Marxist narrative of social progress – that it moved through distinct phases of history from tribalism to feudalism and capitalism, culminating in socialism or communism – was widely accepted. In the 1960s it certainly held great sway across the world as communist countries such as Russia, China, Cuba, North Korea, North Vietnam and the countries of Eastern Europe, based their whole social system on it.

Socialist thinking also dominated the intellectual life of Western Europe and much of the developing world. There, newly empowered leaders in countries as diverse as Ghana, Jamaica and India actively worked toward creating socialist societies of various types – ones that eliminated or marginalised most forms of large-scale private enterprise, and exorcised the demons of global capitalism, and the 19th century colonialism that went with it.

I too was a socialist, or at least a social democrat, and approved of the large-scale nationalisation of the 'commanding heights' of the economy, and thought that we should add banks to the collection of industries that successive British governments had put under state control. While not communists, we British Labour Party supporters wanted the country to be like Sweden, where government dominated the economy and made extensive social provisions.

Private firms such as Volvo existed, particularly in the realm of consumer goods production, but were kept firmly in their place, and were responsive to worker demands for better conditions. Capitalism had to be controlled, it was a system of economic organisation that put profits before people and had no intention of building a fair and just society. It seemed quite right that capitalism and its colonialist multinationals should be sharply curtailed and replaced with a fairer, democratically controlled economic system based on large elements of state planning.

While the moral impulse behind the thinking of the 1960s remains real today, we need to acknowledge that private businesses have been, and remain, really important to the development of human culture around the world. Moore and Lewis point out that multinational businesses were in existence in 2000 BC[5] – they are definitely are not a modern idea:

> "The definition of MNE (multinational enterprise) accepted by the OECD and the UNCTC, 'an enterprise that engages in foreign direct investment (FDI) and owns or controls value-adding activities in more than one country' leads us to conclude that there were MNEs in ancient Assyria around 2000 BC. Characteristics found in modern MNEs such as: hierarchical organisation, foreign employees, value-adding activities in multiple regions, common stock ownership, resource and market seeking behaviour, were

present in these ancient firms. These early MNEs successfully operated considerable business empires in multiple foreign locations from their corporate headquarters in the capital of Ashur."

These private firms played a crucial role in the trading of goods, ranging from raw materials such as tin and copper, foodstuffs, tools and fine ceramics and fabrics, but they were also engaged in manufacturing as well, and fostered various industries around the Middle East. Their activities also supported the growth of the first cities, a development which, in many ways, defines the essence of modern culture. This knowledge of private for-profit commercial activity comes to us from the discovery of about 20,000 clay tablets in Assyrian cuneiform, 85% of which record the economic activities of multinational companies. The disciplines of running a major international enterprise required careful record-keeping and good data, just as it does for modern multinationals today. As Moore and Lewis say, we currently only have access to a small proportion of the clay tablets, and there is a lot more to be learned about these early private firms.

Writing more broadly about the economic and political culture of the region over time, Paul Kriwaczek's book *Babylon*, sets out the historic, economic and social context in which these firms operated. He makes the observation that like us, the early Mesopotamians were experimenting with social systems, to try and manage their political, economic and social life:

"From its mysterious, shadowy beginning until its final, well-documented end, ancient Mesopotamia acted as a kind of experimental laboratory for civilisation, testing, often to destruction, many kinds of religion, from early personifications of natural forces to full blown temple priesthood and even the first stirrings of monotheism; a wider variety of economic and production systems from (their own version) of state planning and centralised direction to (their own style) neo-liberal privatisation, as well as an assortment of government systems, from primitive democracy and consultative monarchy to ruthless tyranny and expansive imperialism. Almost every one of these can be paralleled with similar features found in our own recent history. It sometimes seems as if the whole ancient story served as a dry-run, a dress rehearsal, for the succeeding civilisation, our own, which would originate in the Greece of Periclean Athens after the demise of the last Mesopotamian empire in the sixth century BCE, and which has brought us to where we stand today."[6]

Ancient Mesopotamia wasn't alone in the ancient world in developing private businesses as part of the mix of social institutions. We know that, quite separately in India and China, both cultures had wide-ranging manufacturing and trading activity, and it seems that a variety of 'enterprises' were an integral part of their development. John Browne, former CEO of BP, opens *Connect* – his book on the role of business in society – with a discussion of how the Chinese state and Confucian scholars of the 1st century BC struggled with the social and political implications of the power and wealth of business community and merchants, such that the Chinese state ultimately nationalised strategic enterprises like iron and salt production.[7]

After the fall of the Berlin Wall, I attended a conference in Germany on this historic event and what it meant for the future of society. It was attended by academics, politicians, church leaders, businessmen and others. Late in the second day, the chair noted that no business person had yet spoken and asked for one to come forward. An Indian colleague, who had been sitting next to me, took to the podium and humbly introduced himself as a businessman from Lucknow. He then went on to wryly observe that over four millennia, his city had seen many governments come and go, and many empires too. There had also been many great universities, and a succession of great religions, all of which had left their mark. But throughout that whole time, he said: "The bazaar has always been there". Indeed, it had. The merchants and manufacturers of the bazaar make a vital contribution, for good or ill, to human development.

When Europeans talk about their history, they usually start with Greece and Rome, where private enterprises spread knowledge, culture and religion along with their goods across the empires. Then later in history, nowhere was this activity more evident than across the Muslim world, where the Qur'an helped create a common legal framework for doing business and trade. Goods could flow from Morocco, to India and China, within a common framework of ideas about what constituted a contract, and disputes could be resolved with the help of courts and scholars.

The prophet Muhammad also taught how merchants and businessmen should behave towards each other, and the wider society. The Qur'an, together with Hadith (sayings, actions and pronouncements of the prophet Muhammad that are complementary to the Qur'an), spell out in detail how entrepreneurs should act within the values system of Islam, both as businessmen, but also as members of their community, with a strong emphasis on the giving of charitable contributions.

The Early European Multinationals

Coming more up to date and looking at early modern Europe, we can begin to see why the rampant free market capitalism of the 17th, 18th and 19th centuries was systematically condemned by Marxists and others for its exploitative and colonialist activities. It was the early multinationals of Western Europe, from the early 1600s onwards, that set the scene for the debate about the impact of companies on societies around the world. The Dutch East India Company (VOC), the British East India Company, and later in 1664, the French East India Company, were protomodern multinationals trading between Europe and Asia, with vital connections to the Middle East, Africa and the Americas. It was their activities that created the first global economy and were to create the image of the predatory multinational.

The British East India Company is a good example of these early modern multinationals, and the history of its activities is still very much part of the identity of India, China, and other countries in Asia. Founded in 1601, it was a joint stock company with a monopoly on trade beyond the Cape of Good Hope. It exported bullion to acquire raw materials and goods from Asia, to be sold in Europe, and then on to European settlers in the North American and Caribbean markets. To secure trade and protect their goods, these companies spent heavily on security and, in the early days, fought each other with ships and company troops to control raw materials and markets. The book *Nathaniel's Nutmeg* by Giles Milton[8], describes how the British and the Dutch companies fought each other in 1616 for control of the spice trade from Indonesia. The British lost, and the East India Company went on to focus its future efforts on India.

The British have pretty much forgotten that it was the British East India Company that conquered India, not the British state.[9] The British government only took over the government of India after the great rebellion started by company troops in 1858. Initially, the East India Company traded wonderful goods, such as ceramics ('china' became a global brand name), textiles from India and tea from China.

The drinking of tea was first noted in Britain by Samuel Pepys in 1660. In 1662 the Portuguese princess, Catherine of Braganza, brought the habit to a whole new level in Britain, when she married King Charles II. The custom had been introduced to her home country by Portuguese traders, who had contact with Asia long before the British. Following the example of the new queen, the practice of tea drinking spread rapidly among the wealthy aristocracy, who were following the fashion set by the Court, and could afford to buy this expensive luxury.[10]

Like the taste for tea, the consumption of tropical products such as sugar, coffee, and chocolate was initially confined to the very wealthiest in European society. However, as the East India Company shipped in greater volumes from China, and subsequently India, so the prices came down to create a mass market for tea among the middle class, and then the poor. There were also those that campaigned against this trend because tea was expensive and non-nutritious and it was thought that the poor should not be indulging themselves in this way, and wasting their money.

Tea helped to expand the established market for sugar, in order to sweeten it. However, the widespread consumption and subsequent demand for sugar, and other tropical products such as coffee and tobacco in European and North American markets, required a mass labour force, and the consumption of these products became the key drivers of the Atlantic slave trade. This was a consumer driven crime.

At a time when slavery was found all around the world, businessmen used it to increase production and bring down the prices of products so that the mass market, not just the rich, could enjoy them. This is part of the enduring appeal of capitalism even today: it makes products and services available to the many, not just the few. In the 17th, 18th and 19th centuries, it was tropical foodstuffs, ceramics, clothing, timepieces, coal and other products. Today it's also cars, TVs, mobile phones, computers, credit cards, and internet services, along with experiences like holidays abroad and international travel.

For every product that the rich enjoy today, there is an entrepreneur who wants to spread it to the masses tomorrow, and they will seek to do it by reducing prices and increasing availability. Bringing down prices today often means offshoring production to countries such as China, rather than using slaves, and this modern solution has caused significant social impact in Europe and North America. Here, manufacturing jobs have been lost in traditional industries, while consumers get access to lower-priced products and services.

In his book *The Empire of Things: How We Became a World of Consumers, from the Fifteenth Century to the Twenty-First,*[11] Frank Trentmann points out that by the 1840s, when the British Empire more or less adopted free trade, it became the first empire in history to put the interests of consumers first. The consequences of mass consumption for those producing the goods in Britain and abroad was another matter. They often suffered terribly – such as the slaves producing cotton in the Americas, and the workers in Manchester manufacturing cotton cloth. Friedrich Engels' family had a share in a cotton mill in Manchester; he lived there and saw conditions for workers in the industry and community at first-hand.[12]

The conditions for early factory workers were appalling, both in the workplace, and the environment of the new cities that were springing up around the factories. Children were working 10-hour days in mills for minimal wages, and there was female and child labour in the mines. The writings of Karl Marx, Engels and others, as well as the speeches of Lord Shaftesbury in the British Parliament, give ample testimony to the gross exploitation of labour that accompanied the growth of global capitalism.[13]

The British East India Company serviced consumers in Britain for tea, ceramics, and textiles, but it needed to pay the Chinese in silver for these products, and to earn that silver the Company began selling opium from India to Chinese consumers. This was against the will of the Chinese government, which had its own sources of production, and it tried to ban the imports. In 1840 and 1860, the British East India Company fought two wars with China to enforce free trade and protect the international opium merchants' access to the market.[14] After all, opium could be freely bought in Britain until the end of the 19th century, so why not in China?

Indeed, the Royal Society of Arts and Manufactures offered a reward to encourage the growth of opium in Britain, because it was a powerful medicine, as well as an addictive drug. It was used widely among factory workers, and even Queen Victoria was fond of her opium-based laudanum, to help her cope with the loss of her beloved husband, Albert. Opium consumption in the USA was not controlled until the 1915 Harrison Narcotics Tax Act and it was taken for granted that the masses should have access to it.[15]

In India, the British East India Company discovered wonderful cheap textiles that were soon immensely popular in Britain, and it started to import them wholesale. The British got access to affordable, light and attractive colourful clothing and this was a boom time for Indian textile production. However, the British wool producers and woollen clothing manufacturers were outraged as their trade declined, and they lobbied government to protect their industry, one which had been the very foundation of British exports and wealth accumulation since the Middle Ages.[16] Both Trentmann, and Pietra Rivoli in her book *The Travels of a T-Shirt in the Global Economy*[17], detail the sometimes bizarre laws that were passed to limit the wearing of imported textiles, and promote the wearing of woollen products in Britain. In serving the needs and wants of consumers, with little regard to the economic impact on British producers, the British East India Company was again changing society for good or ill.

Later in the 19th century, technical innovation in Britain meant that India experienced the arrival of cheap, mass-produced and machine-made cotton products from Manchester. These imports of cheap mass-produced cloth helped destroy the livelihood of millions of handloom weavers in India, just as mechanisation had done to handloom weavers in Britain. Absolutely central to the Indian independence struggle was the rejection of cheap, machine-made cloth from Britain because of its impact on domestic spinning and weaving. Vast quantities of imports were burned, and Gandhi himself made spinning and local production of textiles in India central to the independence cause. The original flag of the Indian National Congress also had a spinning wheel at its centre.[18]

The British East India Company was essentially doing what multinationals do today: innovating to service the needs of consumers around the world, and thereby making profits for distribution to its shareholders. It followed the market and, just like today, large groups of producers are often left behind as new sources of production and new technologies replace them. The British East India Company, and the Dutch VOC in particular, helped set the basic pattern of the first global market economy led by consumer demand and shareholder interests. In his book *The Corporation That Changed the World: How the East India Company Shaped the Modern Multinational*,[19] Nick Robins' verdict on the company's 274-year existence is:

> "The East India Company's story is ultimately a tragedy, the tale of an institution that generated great wealth, but also great harm, an institution that was ultimately doomed by the flaws in its corporate design. This story has much to teach the twenty-first century about the dangers of unchecked corporate power and the enduring capacity of people to press for justice."

While the global political and economic context for modern multinationals is radically different from that of the British East India Company – after all, multinationals no longer conquer countries – Robins does make a telling point about corporate governance, which has not changed so radically from the days of what Indians still call 'The Company'. While acknowledging that things are changing, he says:

> "In many countries, such as Britain and India, the sole duty of company directors remains to the company shareholders. In spite of the best intentions of many corporate executives, this legal imperative has a deeply corrosive effect on the way in which companies approach their social responsibilities. In most cases, corporate responsibility becomes a term for enlightened self-interest – that good conduct towards customers, regulators and communities helps to generate a 'licence to operate'. The problem comes, of course, when the interests of the company and society conflict. At this point, corporate responsibility slips into the shadows and the supremacy of shareholder value reasserts itself."

This issue is at the heart of this book: can private companies that are owned by shareholders be good corporate citizens, balancing their rights and responsibilities to all stakeholders, including shareholders, the wider society, and the natural environment? Can we get the benefit of their creativity and organisational ability, while constraining and alleviating their negative impacts?

It was against this background of 19th century global *laissez-faire* capitalism that the 1917 Russian Revolution occurred, where workers and the poor fought back against the injustices of the system. Inspired by Marxist thought, they seized control of the state to build a new society without any form of free enterprise or private companies. As part of wide-ranging reforms, capitalism and the private companies that drove the system were to be abolished, often to be replaced by state-owned enterprises operating within a planned economy. The Russian Revolution set in train a movement that was to dominate intellectual and political life for nearly a century.

Aided by the large-scale failings in the capitalist system, such as the stock market collapse of 1929, and the Great Depression, as well as two world wars, the first global economy collapsed, and the ideas of communism and socialism began to dominate political and intellectual life around the world. Political movements with strong communist, socialist and anti-colonialist tendencies, dominated in the post-war years. Even in Western Europe, political parties of the left were in the ascendency and an anti-business climate prevailed. The USA remained the main spokesperson for a free market economy, but with the Vietnam War and the activities of its multinationals, like the oil giant Aramco in Saudi Arabia, and United Fruit in Central America, it seemed like a continuation of an old order that has had its day.

The Great Change of Direction

The election in 1979 of Margaret Thatcher as Prime Minister in the UK, and in 1981 of Ronald Reagan as the US President, were accompanied by a shift in thinking about the role of private enterprise in the economy and society. These two politicians were determined to reverse the trend of history and confront communist and socialist ideas. They set out to shrink the role of the state, stimulate economic growth, reduce taxes and the regulation of business. They wanted to put private business back at the centre of economic policy and give it the freedom to do what it did well:

deliver a wide range of goods and services, at a low unit cost, to a broad base of consumers.

As the 1980s progressed, theory began to be put into practice, and Mrs Thatcher took the bull by the horns by beginning to denationalise British state-owned industries such as British Rail, British Gas, British Airways, and many more. She turned them into private companies and promoted mass share ownership, while cutting to 40% the top rate of income tax that had been set by the socialist Labour Party at 90% for high earners. President Reagan took a similar approach across the Atlantic with his supply-side economics – he cut tax on top incomes from 70% to 50%. They succeeded in reducing inflation and stimulating economic growth by stimulating private enterprise and, in doing so, set a pattern that the world could not ignore.[20]

Under Deng Xiaoping, who was elected as Paramount Leader of the Chinese People's Republic of China in 1978, the country had also begun to roll back from total state control of the economy, as his Four Modernisations were implemented. China and other countries started to denationalise huge industries and give permission for private enterprises to operate, opening the world economy to a period of rapid change and reintegration. With the collapse of the Berlin Wall in 1989, this trickle of change became a flood. A huge number of private companies were created around the world, and a new era of globalisation was in full swing. Private business was back, and this profound change set the context for this book. The worldwide resurgence of private enterprise posed the question: what is the role of business in our modern global society? What does it mean to be a corporate citizen beyond simply meeting consumer and customer wants and needs, in order to give a return to shareholders?

The 21st century is not the age of the old European colonial companies. Today's companies operate in a much more transparent interconnected world with, in the main, a greater awareness and acknowledgement of their responsibilities to multiple stakeholders, and the natural environment. We have a much better educated populace connected around the globe by the internet and social media, and the actions of companies are under a level of intense scrutiny that was unthinkable a few decades ago. Most importantly, they exist in a very different moral climate from that which prevailed for the British East India Company.

Despite the many differences that exist between countries, peoples, and religions, we now have global values to judge companies by. Most countries have signed up to the Universal Declaration of Human Rights and many of its subsidiary codes and agreements. It clearly says that slavery is wrong, child labour is wrong, women have equal human rights with men, and much more. Businesses today operate around the world in a very different moral climate, one with much clearer global standards of behaviour. Above all, there is that scrutiny by stakeholders, the media, and others, which was impossible in the days when it took six months to get a letter from the London headquarters of the East India Company to its offices in Calcutta.

Free Enterprise's Other Critics

Communists and socialists are the most significant critics of free enterprise, because they sought to capture state power, and use it to eliminate or seriously constrain private enterprise. However, they are not the only groups that have grave concerns about the role of business in society and the power it wields. On the far right, the Fascist Party in Italy, and the Nazi Party in Germany (National Socialist Workers' Party of Germany), had mixed relations with business at best. The Nazis were socialists after all, and seized state power to control the economy and society, including businesses. In his book *The Wages of Destruction: The Making and Breaking of the Nazi Economy*[21], Adam Tooze says of the Nazi party's coming to power in 1932, with the Great Depression raging:

> "Now capitalism's deepest crisis left German business powerless to resist a state intervention that came not from the left but the right. The first years of Hitler's regime saw the imposition of a series of controls on German business that were unprecedented in peace time history."

Wages, prices and dividends were all controlled, and industries that supported the party line on autarky (self-sufficiency) and rearmament, such as chemicals and steel, were favoured, while others, such as textiles, which required foreign cotton and other raw materials, were forced into decline. Large numbers of companies were forced to reorganise and join government-sponsored cartels.

The Nazi Party did not want an alternative centre of power in society, acting in ways that the Party did not approve of, such as being owned by or employing Jews, importing foreign products, or making contraceptives, which was one of the first businesses to be banned. While the leadership of large companies that benefited from Nazi economic policies, such as Krupp (steel and armaments) and IG Farben (chemicals, synthetic rubber and fabrics), supported the Nazis, others were less fortunate. Tooze describes the situation of Dr Hugo Junkers, owner of the largest aircraft industry in Germany, who was arrested for treason and forced to hand over his business to the state:

> "His difficulty was simply that he owned the largest aircraft plant in Germany and that Goering and his Secretary of State Erhard Milch were determined to have control of it."

Anti-business rhetoric and action has long had a place in populist movements of the right, but not to the same degree as the left; the nationalist right tend to accept business as agents of the market while they go about organising the economy, to serve the national interest, as they define it.

The great secular ideologies of the 20th century, communism and fascism, are not the only movements opposed to, or suspicious of, business. They both sought state power to control the economy and society, but there are those that live within the free market system but are still potentially very critical of it. For example, Christian religious groups and other religious traditions have a long-standing critique of business and seek to influence it through the exercise of ethical judgment. For Christians, there is enough anti-business sentiment in the New Testament to justify firmly controlling the activities of businesses, and the bankers without the aid of Marxist thought. After all, the only act of violence attributed to Jesus of Nazareth was to whip the money lenders trading in the temple grounds, and he taught that it was easier for a camel to pass through the eye of a needle than for a rich man to enter heaven.

Throughout its history, Christianity, like Islam, has had a strong prohibition against usury, and today's Christian leaders are still likely to be critics of business. *Dethroning Mammon: Making Money Serve Grace,*[22] the latest book by the Archbishop of Canterbury, Justin Welby, is a good example of this tradition. This is not that surprising, after all, for each of the seven deadly sins, there seems to be a capitalist enterprise catering for it: greed, lust, gluttony, sloth, wrath, envy and pride. Not to mention that selling alcohol, tobacco, and gambling are all well provided for in the free market of the West.

In the USA, where people have always accepted the free market as the medium of production and exchange, the behaviour of business is still actively scrutinised from an ethical perspective, and the roots of that ethical discourse are still firmly planted in religious thought and experience. Religious groups play an important role in US society by questioning business policy and behaviour. The same is true in many cultures of the world, no more so than in Muslim countries, where business is held accountable to the clear guidance given in the Qur'an and Hadith. Indeed, in rapidly developing Muslim countries such as Malaysia, and elsewhere in the Muslim world, there is an urgent discourse on the role of business in modern society. Can economic development be squared with religious teachings? That is often a difficult question for conservative religious scholars, who seek to constrain the human propensity to sin.

However, Christian religious teaching was never just about criticising business but, like Islam, also about shaping business behaviour in a positive way. In Northern Europe, Max Weber argued in his book *The Protestant Ethic and the Spirit of Capitalism*[23], and Richard Tawney in his book *Religion and the Rise of Capitalism*[24], that the Protestant Reformation led to a change in religious thinking about economics, and the importance of profits in particular.

They argue that this change was in fact fundamental to the rise of modern capitalism in that part of the world and the USA. Indeed, drawing on their Christian faith, some Protestant businessmen built successful businesses known for their honesty in pricing, fair treatment of workers, suppliers, customers and communities alike, including the Quaker firms of Cadbury and Rowntree. In his book *Family Capitalism*[25], Harold James shows that many owners of large 19th century enterprises in Europe were motivated by Catholic social teaching to introduce policies to provide for workers and the community.

Whatever the reader might think about the role of religion in society generally, all types and denominations had a role in articulating the values by which human beings should treat each other. This can be seen in the behaviour of the owners of some 19th century businesses. Like Robert Owen at the start of the Industrial Revolution, some saw their work in business as a trust, one that had a social value far beyond a simple economic transaction, and their beliefs were a key force in shaping their behaviour towards their workers and other stakeholders within their own businesses. However, their approach was not widely adopted, as systemic problems with the capitalist system led to the rise of communism and socialism.

Another group critical of business that exists in Western society at least, is a school of thought that focuses on the important things in life being done 'for their own sake'. Classically these views are held by intellectuals and artists, who see philosophy, science and a wide range of arts as the ultimate expression of human life – the highest aspiration of culture. Things done for the 'market' are of a much lower level of cultural value. In her book *Among the Bohemians: Experiments in Living 1900-1939* [26], Virginia Nicholson gives a clear account of how a movement that started in the late 19th century with the Bloomsbury Group fostered a modern separation between cultural life and business.[27] To some extent, the hippies of the 1960s picked up the mantle of these upper-class intellectuals and, as trend-setters in their own time did much to foster an anti-corporate ethos in society.

This constituency is important because artists and others are influential in shaping trends in politics and the wider culture through ideas, books, films, other art forms and the media. They are inclined to disdain the profit motive, and feel human needs and wants should be met without the workings of the market. Engaging in commercial activity is definitely to be avoided. However, their ideas are often picked up by business, particularly in fashion and media, and turned into profitable activities. Many of these 'social innovators' and 'creatives' – unless they benefit from family trust funds – are also tied into the market economy. In reality, musicians, actors and artists, wanting a good financial return for their work, avidly seek to protect their intellectual property rights and get a fair return from their labour. After all, they are entitled to it.

Finally, business has to contend with the scrutiny of the other powerful agency in modern society, a free press. It is a vital part of the social mix of Western capitalism, which since the days of the muck-raking journalists in the USA taking on the business practices of the 'robber baron' capitalists, has done much to expose corporate malfeasance. Companies are far from perfect, and external criticism is vital to keeping their assumptions and behaviour under review. The lack of a critical free press in some former communist countries like Russia and China, that have embraced private enterprise, is a matter of concern as companies take an ever growing share of economic power.

However, while this role for the formal media still exists in print and electronic media such as radio and TV, it has been greatly amplified by the emergence of social media, which is now totally global in character. For example, a child labour scandal in the business of a central African supplier can be front page news in London, with pictures, within 24 hours, all courtesy of a concerned citizen, equipped with a smartphone, who may well work for a campaigning non-profit. These individuals and organisations were critical in shaping business practices in the past when they campaigned against the slave trade, and they remain very important today.

Business Responds to the New World Order

For its part, business has quickly adapted to take advantage of the political and economic changes that began in the 1980s and 1990s. With the opening of global markets, trade shot up from less than 30% of world GDP in the early 1980s to about 60% by 2007, and despite the financial crash, it remains there today. New consumers, sources of labour, and raw materials were suddenly abundant, as the former communist and socialist world opened up.

However, business has been much less vigorous in defining a new role for itself in modern society, and there is a lot of getting back to business as usual. Indeed, there has also been a certain element of triumphalism in some quarters and a lazy acceptance of the 'new world order' as being a reassertion of the pre-communist natural order of things. Business is back in a global marketplace, but has not yet fully found its place as a 'citizen' in modern society: a role which recognises a company's contribution and value as a commercial entity, but acknowledges its wider role in society.

This situation is in large part its own fault. With a few exceptions, business leaders have not thought through, nor accepted responsibility for, the great economic, social and environmental changes that global commercial activities are unleashing. When they gather at Davos, and are free from the day-to-day concerns of running a business, company leaders struggle with this issue. They know that surveys such as the Edelman *Trust Barometer* which is regularly presented, show low levels of trust in business.

The business leaders know that if they follow the market and shift production to China to save costs, or develop new products such as robots and driverless trucks, they will be undermining the livelihoods of workers in developed countries. And these workers may well react unfavourably as voters, as the election of President Trump and Britain's vote to leave the EU seem to show. Looking to the future, while learning lessons from the past, business leaders are aware of the problems associated with the 'creative destruction' of capitalism. They can see the old patterns reasserting themselves around the world and discuss issues at a high level of generalisation, which is important because not all issues facing society can be dealt with at the level of the individual enterprise, but they will need to be involved in providing solutions.

In its reporting of a discussion at Davos in January 2017, where business leaders were considering the emerging economic and social impact of artificial intelligence and robotics, the *Financial Times* says[28]:

> "…a clear message from many panels devoted to AI at the WEF is that technology is advancing much faster than anticipated. 'The speed at which AI is advancing is beyond even the most optimistic people,' said Kai-fu Lee, a venture capitalist with Sinovation Ventures and a former Google and Microsoft executive in China. 'Pretty much anything that requires 10 seconds of thinking or less can soon be done by AI or algorithms.'

> "That is making the debate about how to handle the huge profits generated by the elimination of millions of jobs more urgent as well."

Blue-collar jobs are on the line, as they have been since the 1980s. For example, America's 8.7 million truckers are facing the licensing of the first ever self-driving truck in Nevada. If that trend takes off, then one of the last bastions of well-paid blue-collar work will fall. In addition, AI and other innovations, along with outsourcing, are starting to replace white-collar jobs too. The West Coast entrepreneur, and icon of modern capitalism, Elon Musk, the founder of Tesla and SpaceX, is quoted in *The Times*[29] of London as saying:

> "There will be fewer and fewer jobs that a robot cannot do better (than humans),' the billionaire told a summit in Dubai. 'These are not things I wish will happen; they are things I think will probably happen. And if my assessment is correct, we are going to have to think about it? I think some kind of universal basic income is going to be necessary. The output of goods and services will become extremely high. With automation there will come abundance. Almost everything will get very cheap.'

> "Mr Musk, 45, has reservations, however. He said: 'The harder challenge is how are people to have meaning? A lot of people derive their meaning from their employment. So, if there is no need for your labour, what's your meaning? Do you feel useless? That's a much harder problem to deal with.'"

Elon Musk is musing on the idea of a state salary for everyone as a result of corporate innovation. This is an idea championed by the radical left and demonstrates how even business people struggle with the consequences of this new wave of global creativity being unleashed by the resurgent private sector. The theoretical solutions to these pending changes are many and could include raising taxes generally, or tax on robots specifically to create jobs in the state sector, or allow more funding for a rapid growth of jobs in the non-profit sector. It is fine for business leaders to have general ideas about the economy and society, but what are their individual businesses doing about the issues? That is a central challenge of this book.

In the 1980s, when Levi's faced its first ever wave of plant closures, consumers would not pay the price of a pair of jeans made in the USA. Competition in the marketplace was intense and the company started to contract. Today Levi's, which once had more than 20,000 employees worldwide in the 1980s, now owns and operates no factories. It is no longer a manufacturing company and the generation of management that opened plants in America's southern states in the 1950s and successfully confronted the issue of racism in employment, was replaced by one which had to close them.

It was a large part of my job at the company in the 1980s to help the communities affected by plant closures to find new and more modern sources of employment beyond the garment industry. The company recognised the reality that garment production is very much an 'entry level' industry for developing countries and societies, and that in developed countries such as the USA or in Europe, the future for workers was to move up to jobs with higher levels of productivity. It owned its share of the problem and devoted time and modest resources to helping solve it, often in partnership with the leadership of the affected communities and non-profits, with the skill to help them. As the wheel of industrial life turned yet again, the company showed good citizenship in responding to the changes. It did not sit on the side lines wringing its hands about the unavoidable changes of the market economy.

The creativity and inventiveness of for-profit sector companies is a wonderful thing, but they can also have unpleasant consequences for many, particularly displaced producers, and this has been true since the days of the East India Company and the emergence of the Industrial Revolution. Let companies face that fact and plan to do something about it, not only in public discussion but at the level of the individual enterprise. They don't have to do it all alone if they pitch in with governments and non-profits. The truly global aspect of these changes is also a key factor and national governments cannot necessarily cope with global forces that have intense local impacts in multiple jurisdictions. In many ways, multinational companies are much better placed to see worldwide trends and consequently make an informed contribution to the local response.

CHAPTER 2:

The Resurgent For-Profit Sector

Why Did It Make a Comeback?

World history has moved in a new direction since the elections of Margaret Thatcher in 1979, Ronald Reagan in 1981, and the fall of the Berlin Wall in 1989. Why this happened is important to acknowledge, and there is no single reason. From the end of the Second World War, the communist, socialist and social democratic left, along with the leadership of many of the newly independent countries of the global south, had many 'progressive' economic, social and political agendas. These included social justice and progress, including greater equality for women, the provision of jobs and of services for the people such as education, healthcare and social services, and establishing truly independent countries away from economic and other forms of control by the old colonial powers.

Countries such as Cuba and China achieved a lot in these areas, but communist and socialist regimes also promised prosperity and economic growth to fund new provisions and entitlements. For a short while during the post-war years, it seemed that communism would be a more efficient mechanism than capitalism, producing the goods and services in which all people would share. For many years, China benchmarked its production of steel against that of the old colonial power Britain and, like Russia, India and many other newly independent countries, it was determined to do much better than the capitalists and take a great economic leap forward.

A planned economy seemed self-evidently a much more effective one than a wasteful capitalist one that produces 50 types of car, when only one or two were logically necessary. In addition, on the left, there was a sense of moral decadence and vanity in this type of extensive consumer choice. A car was there to do a job, to move people from A to B, so why pander to the consumer's aspirational tastes? Consequently, while West Germany developed the Audi and the BMW, communist East Germany had the rather sad little Trabant. At the point of reunification in 1990, West Germany had a GDP per head more than twice that of East Germany and while that is not the only measure of a society's success (East Germany had much better rates of participation of women in the workforce and the child care to support them than the West), the people of the East firmly rejected communism.

There are many reasons why communism collapsed and socialism retreated, and I have yet to read anything compelling by a leftist on why it happened. Communism was pretty good at big infrastructure projects such as building dams, and the Soviet Union led the space race in the 1950s and 1960s, but totalitarianism, paternalistic authoritarianism and bureaucracy, together with the denial of freedom and free expression, all undermined people's belief in the 'project'. The Soviet Union found it difficult to match President Reagan's military spending, while its great writers and poets were suppressed because they did not follow the party line – and that alienated intellectuals and artists around the world. Also banning the Beatles and Levi's as subversive, decadent influences was not a good idea if you wanted to keep the mass of young people on side.

The people of the socialist world also began to want access to consumer goods of modern life such as fridges, washing machines, TVs, record players and telephones, interesting food, medicine, clothing and more personal experiences such as foreign travel. All of which were in short supply in their countries. The communists were trying to improve people's standard of living, and providing public services such as health, education and public transport, but they did not do a good job in providing for personal consumer choice. These products came to symbolise much of the Western lifestyle, but because of the repressive totalitarian nature of communist regimes, and their planned economies, people could not voice their discontent or influence the products available through their spending.

Box 1

There is an old joke that sums up this aspect of this conflict between West and East in the following way. When President Roosevelt of the USA and Joseph Stalin of Russia met in Yalta for the first time, they were keen to get on and part of the conversation went something like this:

Stalin said: "Mr Roosevelt, I don't think the people of the USA understand that the mission of the Communist Party is to bring freedom, justice and prosperity to the masses of people. Let me send a copy of the Communist Manifesto to every home in the USA, and I will let you send one book to every home in the Soviet Union. Come on, Franklin, what do you say?"

Roosevelt thought for a moment and replied: "OK, Joe, it's a deal!"

Stalin said: "Good, good! What book is it you will be sending to my people?"

Roosevelt replied: "I thought I would send them the Sears Catalogue."

To people in the communist and socialist countries, all well drilled in its many shortcomings, liberal capitalism still had characteristics that were appealing. The free market economy was clearly associated with freedom of both political and personal expression. It generally existed alongside some sort of democracy in the West, and it also steadily delivered on the promise to improve people's material lives. The free market system did not give people a five-year plan to increase car and TV production, it just did it by harnessing the creative and productive power of thousands of private companies. Whatever the reason for the collapse of the communist and socialist project, one thing stands out: the inventiveness of capitalism progressively gives ordinary people access to a wide range of goods and services that can enrich their everyday lives.

Ordinary people often supported socialism because it was a way of achieving a better life through collective action and it provided social stability and jobs, for example. They wanted a share of the power held by the rich elites, so they wanted to take over government. They wanted a share of the culture that the elites had, so they wanted access to education and the arts. They also wanted the healthcare that the rich have, so they supported public spending on clinics, hospitals and healthcare.

However, they also wanted the 'stuff' of life that the rich had: the food and drink, the clothes and shoes, the consumer products like cars, mobile phones, the credit cards, the air travel and more. In the post-war years, Western companies were doing just what the British East India Company did in its day – bringing down the prices of 'elite' consumer products so that the poor could access them. A company such as Unilever today is giving a family in Bangladesh all the soap and other products it needs for personal use and laundry, for the price of a can of Coca-Cola.

There are those who condemn this trend as promoting individualistic consumerism, while environmentalists worry, with good reason, about the burden that consumption places on the planet's resources. However, the fact remains that all around the world, poor people are looking to acquire the goods and services that the private sector offers. People want the 'stuff' that is considered a normal part of modern life, and if they don't have it, they feel deprived. Even socialist India, which for many years had a small range of cars based on the British Morris Minor, eventually turned to the Tata Company to help produce the Nano, a people's car for newly empowered consumers.

Those in the non-profit world who want to solve the problem of poverty must accept that when the poor have money, they are going to spend their disposable income as they like, most probably on some of the products and services of modern business. Some poor men may well want a beer and a T-shirt, while their wives might well buy things for the home and the children, such as toothpaste, shampoo and books. In addition, many of the poor are going to make their way out of poverty by starting a small business and generating a sustainable income from selling their goods or services in the marketplace. They won't be relying on government subsidies and handouts from charities, they will be working within a market-based system to create their own income. While some may criticise the behaviour of large companies, but not these startups and small ventures, they need to recognise that both will be working within exactly the same context of consumer and customer-led production.

Wealth Creation Matters

The for-profit sector is the world's great wealth-creating engine, and it is that reality that has done so much to promote the return of private business around the world. The economic activity of the for-profit sector creates the products and services that people need and want. Its profits are the major source of global investment capital, as well as being used to support pension funds. Its activity creates jobs for employees and suppliers and gives government taxes, to mention just a few of its economic contributions. Above all, its economic activity drives growth and development in a way that government economic control does not, and that is not only in relation to consumer goods, but in infrastructure projects and financial services too.

While government has been shedding jobs, the for-profit and non-profit sectors have been creating them, paying wages and providing benefits to millions of workers around the world. Companies not only support livelihoods directly but also indirectly through their value chains, backward to raw material producers and forward in paths to market, including small retail shops. A whole new world of workers in manufacturing and farming has been brought into the global economy through the extensive supply chains that international companies create. The products they bring to the market change everyday lives and very often make them more productive, whether that's through the mobile phone, computer, the washing machine or the microwave.

At the same time, companies are earning foreign currency and paying national and local taxes in many forms: corporation tax, employment and local taxes, taxes on legal transactions and insurance, plus the sales and excise taxes collected by consumer goods companies. When companies close down or move their production off-shore, whole cities, such as Detroit, can be devastated because the local economy no longer has industry to create the wealth that gave the community life. The activities of private firms are a vital part of our life in society, but are not uncontroversial.

There are non-profits that campaign on corporate taxes, corruption and bribery, human rights at work and in the supply chain, consumer rights and product safety. Trade unions have been in the business of campaigning for workers' rights since the earliest days of the Industrial Revolution. Unions want good and safe working conditions but, most particularly, they seek a larger share of the wealth that the firm creates to come back to its members via wages and pensions. They are not wrong to do this and often have good points to make, but they are arguing over the way that the wealth companies produce is distributed. You need to be able to create the wealth before you can distribute it.

This process of corporate wealth creation has, in the past 40 years, been unleashed on a global scale. As Joseph Schumpeter says when discussing the 'creative destruction' of capitalism in his book *Capitalism, Socialism and Democracy*:[30]

> "The essential point to grasp is that in dealing with capitalism we are dealing with an evolutionary process. It may seem strange that anyone can fail to see so obvious a fact which moreover was long ago emphasized by Karl Marx. Yet that fragmentary analysis which yields the bulk of our propositions about the functioning of modern capitalism persistently neglects it...Capitalism, then is by nature a form or method of economic change and not only never is but never can be stationary...The fundamental impulse that sets and keeps the capitalist engine in motion comes from the new consumers' goods, the new methods of production or transportation, the new markets, the new forms of industrial organization that capitalist enterprise creates."

New products, new ways of manufacturing, and sourcing of production from the formerly closed labour markets of China, India and Eastern Europe have, among other factors, had a hugely disruptive effect on the world economy. This disruption is resented by those who suffer from it as they see their factories closed and jobs go abroad, for example. On the other hand, consumers have benefited from new products such as iPhones and cheap goods, ranging from clothes and shoes, to cars and foreign holidays. The creativity of the for-profit sector is immense but it frightens people because they don't know where it is leading, and they worry about it repeating patterns from the past.

For example, the 2008 financial crash nearly bankrupted the whole world economy (thank goodness government was there to step in and save the bankers from themselves), and people know that financial crashes are nothing new in capitalism; they have happened regularly since the days of the South Seas Bubble. The 2008 crash, even though it was in the bond market, did echo the stock market crash of 1929, and it seems like a repeating pattern. It showed clearly how closely the global financial markets, as well as the market for goods, are now firmly linked, and that even major governments have difficulty in influencing them.

The rapid integration of the global economy since 1989 is an example of the creativity of private firms. When opportunities open up, they step right in to exploit them, to find new markets, sources of investment, raw materials and labour. While global integration is not new, the speed at which it has been accomplished is. The modern means of communication through the internet in particular, underpins the rapid speed of change, and this rate of change also frightens people. In addition, while people are welcoming the new wealth, goods and services that free enterprise is bringing them, a new concern has emerged. People are increasingly aware that while capitalism may be far more inclusive than the Marxist ever thought possible, it probably cannot pay the environmental price of its success.

The Profit Motive Drives a Connection With Human Needs and Wants

The for-profit sector is huge in scale and very diverse. It is made up of a wide range of players, from self-employed consultants and small businesses, ,to mid-sized national companies and global multinationals, some privately held family firms, or publicly quoted ones. Some are consumer-facing, while many others are engaged in business to business transactions. However, the basic rule of the game in this sector is that income must exceed expenditure and the firm must be able to make a profit to survive. Some firms exist because income and expenditure just about match and they survive, giving the owners a modest livelihood. Other private firms must make a sufficient surplus or profit to pay back bank loans and give shareholders a return on their investment, so they need a higher rate of return on the capital employed.

The need to make a profit forces the company to listen to its consumers and customers. A company must meet their needs and wants, or go out of business. The profit motive drives a close connection between the business and its consumers and customers, and in a competitive free market environment, customers and consumers have choices about who they will do business with.

One of the big problems for the planned economies was that the government-owned enterprises did not heed clear signals from the marketplace about what customers and consumers needed and wanted. State enterprises were mandated to produce a certain number of consumer goods to meet projected demand, but the design and quality were often stipulated top-down from managers. They often did not respond to what the consumer wanted or aspired to have in the same careful way for-profit companies do.

The question of profit is the defining issue for this sector, and one that continues to cause a great deal of concern and discussion in society. There is still a popular view that one man's profit is another's loss and, most important, that the basic role of business is to *maximise* profits or returns. This proposition is agreed on by thinkers as diverse as Karl Marx, Milton Friedman and Joseph Stiglitz, and is widely taught in universities and business schools. It is a key underlying assumption in many economic and social theories – they don't really work without it, but from the companies I have worked with, I doubt that they seek to do this in practice.

It is clearly the case that profit maximisation goes on in the for-profit sector and the marketplace, and it would be foolish to deny it. For example, whether day trading on the stock market, individuals selling houses and cars, or big companies with monopolies and unique products, they all want to get the maximum they can within a competitive marketplace. However, for a business with long-term customers and consumers which has survived for over 100 years, it has not done so by maximising profits. These companies *optimise* their profits over time. If a company wants repeat business, not just a one-off sale, it needs to pay careful regard to the interests of its customers, consumers and indeed a wider range of stakeholders.

If a company exists purely to maximise profits, there is very little room for a discussion of corporate citizenship. However, if it is optimising profits over time, then the issue of good citizenship is an important part of the discussion. A key reason being that management has to balance the interests of a range of stakeholders, and do so while giving shareholders a 'sound' or 'fair' return, not a maximum one, as the Johnson & Johnson Credo says in Box 2 Chapter 7.

In my view, most large companies in the 'real economy', providing goods and services to customers and consumers, are long-term profit optimisers. By 'real economy' I am talking about companies that make things, or otherwise contribute to offering society goods and services in the marketplace. In addition to making a profit, these companies have multiple points of contact with society, and need good relations with customers, consumers, suppliers, governments and communities to survive and thrive. These vital relationships limit radical profit maximisation, and they put a premium on optimising profits with regard to the interests of other stakeholders.

This book is concerned with these sorts of businesses. They are the large and small 'agents' of the market. They have choices about their decisions and behaviour, and the range of those choices would be very limited if their role is purely to maximise profits for shareholders and owners. In the real world, where major companies optimise profits over time, it is possible to have a dialogue about ethical behaviour and social and environmental responsibility. This is a conversation about the long-term success of the business in a changing society; one where the attitudes and behaviour of companies are as important as the attitudes and behaviour of individuals in society. More so, if one considers the scale, complexity and global reach of companies.

Governments and Non-Profits Are in Business

One of the reasons why private business is back is that the idea of the 'enterprise' never really went away. It is important to appreciate that business and profit-making activity are not just the preserve of the private for-profit sector. Governments in communist societies were opposed to privately owned businesses, but they in turn owned and operated vast state enterprises. Even today in the post-Thatcher era, governments around the world have a direct involvement in developing and running businesses. It is not just a capitalist thing, the communists took over private enterprises and often just made them state-owned enterprises. These state-owned enterprises still exist in vast numbers and are active in many economic sectors around the world, extracting raw materials, generating power, providing water, airlines and telecoms, to name but a few.

From my experience, these government-owned businesses are noticeably absent from debates about corporate citizenship. There seems to be an implicit assumption that if a state runs a business, that it is serving the people, not exploiting them, by making profits. Government-owned businesses often make a profit or a 'surplus', but if the business doesn't do well, it is assumed that governments will pump in subsidies from taxation to support it. Mrs Thatcher thought that this practice was basically immoral, and her central political policy was based on the idea that private companies run businesses better than governments, and that is why she wanted them brought back to play a central role in society.

In the West, the hostility to private firms is often based on their profit-making, which is seen as their primary purpose and perceived as driving any amount of bad behaviour. For example, the sale of harmful products such as tobacco by private firms is roundly criticised by many, including some investors, as being unethical. It always comes as a shock to young people to learn that the largest tobacco company in the world is the China National Tobacco Corporation, which is owned and operated by that enemy of profit and friend of the people, the Chinese Communist Party. It has 89 brands and produces about 30% of all the cigarettes made on the planet. Consequently, China has about 350 million smokers and one of the worst records of lung cancer globally. Until about 10 years ago, the Japanese government owned the national tobacco company, as do other governments around the world, while hundreds of millions of cigarettes are produced in the informal economy in countries such as India.

When we consider alcohol production and distribution, it is mainly in the private sector in the West where companies face extensive criticism for their manufacturing, pricing and marketing policies. Even so, Diageo plc estimates that about 63% of the sale of a bottle of Smirnoff vodka goes to the government in tax, 27% in production and marketing and 10% to the retailer. While the British government, like many others in the West, is not directly involved in producing and distributing alcohol, it takes a huge amount of tax from the industry it licences and regulates.

The largest alcoholic beverages company in the world is in fact owned by the Russian government which, despite liberalising control, still has about 65% of the market for consumption, which in Russia is one of the highest per capita in the world. Consequently, Russia has some really serious alcohol related problems that are in many respects worse than in the free market West. Even the socially progressive Swedish government is a major producer of vodka, while the Canadian government controls retail distribution.

In the non-profit sector, there are a number of monasteries producing wonderful liqueurs, and one of the favourite tipples of London street drinkers for many years was a strong brew nicknamed 'Buckie'. At 15% alcohol, it was originally produced by a religious order based at Buckfast Abbey in England, and is now produced under licence by a private firm. There was even a chain of non-profit pubs called "Goths" in Britain, which was set up to promote responsible drinking. They have faded away over time, but represent an early attempt to use business activity to address a social problem by regulating drinking.

In developing countries such as Ghana, the formal private sector production of beer and spirits represents only about 20% of all the alcohol consumed in the country. What dominates the market is informal sector production, where the spirit Akpeteshie and palm wine are produced by small informal sector producers for local consumption. This form of production is often not regulated and taxed, and quality control is poor, which has led to periodic incidences of death and blindness. Consequently, developing countries' governments have a huge incentive to bring it into the formal sector, where it can be taxed and regulated. This was the case in 18th century Britain, when the gin epidemic led government to regulate informal sector production and tax it.

Government can of course decide to ban alcohol, as the USA did in 1920, when campaigning non-profits finally triumphed and pressured government to close down the production of alcohol for about 13 years. There are states in India that still aspire to prohibition and some devout Muslim countries such as Saudi Arabia still ban its production and sale altogether. However, even that country still struggles to control its consumption and some governments have chosen to produce and distribute alcohol as a means of controlling the business 'for the public good'. Others just take a large cut from the activities of private companies and let them suffer the opprobrium of being the producer. Either way, the consumers' strong desire for alcoholic beverages gets met, governments, government-owned businesses, private businesses and even non-profits bow to it.

When it comes to the non-profit sector where campaigning non-governmental organisations (NGOs) are often the most hostile to business, it is important to note that many such entities are themselves directly involved in business as a means of raising funds. A major charity such as Oxfam has a trading arm that produces income to support its charitable activities. In 2016, total trading sales produced £85.9m out of a total unrestricted income of £169m, and why not? It is a good thing that charities can secure their independence by having income-generating businesses that pass their profits back to the charity to support its wider social mission.[31] Oxfam, Christian Aid and many other charities also do much to promote small business activities and the self-reliance that comes from them in the developing world. They see these small businesses as a route out of poverty, and many of them become successful as suppliers to larger Western businesses, producing food or flowers, for example.

Similarly, if government wants to run various types of business, why not? As long as the business is well run and gives the people goods or services they need. My point is not ideological, it is practical. The British Labour Party has said that it wants to renationalise the railways, so let them; the consumer will judge the product and make their views known in various ways. What matters here is that all enterprises, whoever owns them, need to have a citizenship agenda. The point is that the government, non-profit and indeed informal sectors are much closer to companies in terms of dealing with the economic, social and environmental challenges of business activity than they acknowledge. The big difference is that private for-profit firms distribute their profits to owners and shareholders, whereas the other sectors don't, and that is why profits are still controversial.

Business is More Than Just Making Profits

Again, it is important to acknowledge that business is not just about making a profit. There are many reasons why people set up businesses and work for them that have nothing to do with profits. People in private companies often like the freedom, opportunity for creativity and power that comes from this independence. Furthermore, there are businesses that start and grow because they have a social mission.

My home town of Nottingham in the British East Midlands, was host to a business started by the Boot family, which had experience of using herbal treatments when living out in the country.[32] Once settled in Nottingham, they started an informal business to help local people with their illnesses. This ultimately led to the establishment of a formal business, Boot Cash Chemists, which competed with other chemists in the town by providing plainly wrapped products for cash, at the lowest possible prices. As he asked his customers for cash, Jesse Boot paid his suppliers in cash and developed a firm reputation for honest dealing.

In the 1870s, Jesse Boot did not campaign for government to start a national health service to solve the problem, nor did he set up a charity to give medicines away. He founded a business and sold people what they needed at a fair price. His shop was in one of the poorest parts of town and he lived close to the people he served. As the business grew, he became wealthy, a bit like many of the early Quaker businessmen who weren't looking to become rich when they set up their businesses, but rather to serve the community. In fact, the accumulation of wealth was somewhat embarrassing to them and they were well known for giving it away. Jesse Boot did the same and went on to found the city university. It was the success of Boots that gave Nottingham the university, not the state, and it remains a prime example of good citizenship in the community.

There are many examples of businesses following this trend around the world. In India, the Tata Company, initially founded in 1868, grew under successive members of the family and sought to usher India into the industrial age with its first locally owned steel plant, hydroelectric and other projects.[33] The company was not just to make a profit for shareholders but to be part of the positive act of 'nation-building' for India, one which required it to have the highest standards of ethical and socially responsible behaviour towards workers and other stakeholders. That motive is still important to many business leaders in the developing world today as they see their businesses contributing to the development of their country. In many ways the same can be said of Andrew Carnegie's investments in the

USA in the 1870s, where he made the steel that built the country's railways and bridges and bound the country together.[34]

People set up businesses to meet needs and wants in the community just as others set up non-profits for a similar purpose. The issues they address will differ, and many activities in the community will never be profitable, but it can be surprising what is. In his book *Poor No More*[35], Peter Cove describes his transition from activist and government-funded community worker, active with the poor and unemployed who he saw as victims of the 'capitalist system'. However, he became disillusioned with government welfare programmes and charity-based approaches to those in poverty and, with his wife, set up a for-profit company called America Works. It is operating in territory that is normally the preserve of the other two sectors and despite, or perhaps because of, being rewarded on a payment-by-results system, the business has proved a success with about 700,000 people being helped into jobs. The profit motive is not a bar to social service; in some cases, it can be just another route to achieving it.

CHAPTER 3:

The Rise of a Global Social System

Private Companies Help Complete the Mix of Social Institutions

In this chapter we look in detail at the three organised sectors of the modern world (government, for-profit and non-profit). The re-emergence of the private for-profit sector around the world has helped complete a viable mix of organised sectors that together, have a far better chance of meeting all the needs, wants and aspirations of humanity, than government alone. Each sector, including the for-profit sector, brings something special to the social mix. In my view, a civilised society needs all three sectors to be vibrant and effective and to do well, each offering society distinctive life-enhancing opportunities.

Government is, in principle, providing security, law, infrastructure, education, healthcare and other services for the people. In theory, it exists to serve the people, not just the governing elite. The non-profit sector or civil society sector, with its wide range of charities and community organisations, also exists to serve the people but with a passion that state bureaucracies sometimes find it difficult to muster.

However, the for-profit sector is seen as being there to serve profit, and profit is a suspect word all around the world. If someone is profiting, many feel that someone else must be losing out. This zero-sum game is reminiscent of a world where the universal cake of wealth was permanently fixed, and the fight was all about who got what share. Today, business is the major force that is growing that economic cake and, while there is still a fight to be had about how it is shared out, the major force for economic growth and often social change in our lives is the for-profit sector. It is often tolerated, but not at all loved, or even appreciated, by many. It has an uneasy place in a modern society's mix of institutions, and we need to learn how better to live with it.

The situation is, of course, much more complex than these few comments but, simply put, the for-profit sector does make an immense contribution to society through its activities, and while the profit motive is central to its existence, it is not the sum total of what it is about. It also serves people as consumers, workers, investors, suppliers and other stakeholders such as government and communities, which are desperate for its jobs, taxes and local investment, but it also needs to play a role as a citizen in meeting the immense challenges that humanity faces.

The emergence of a global social structure based on three formal sectors, frames our discussion of modern corporate citizenship, and specifically how private companies fit into it. This pattern of institutions has developed because taken together, the three sectors meet a wider range of people's needs and aspirations than any one sector alone. It has emerged almost unconsciously over the past 40 years. While in itself, it does not offer a solution to society's problems, it does offer a way of working through them. Each component has its part to play because none of the single sectors has all the solutions. The challenge now is how to make this emergent system work. As Winston Churchill said of democracy: "It is the least worst system we have got".

Around the world, partly by choice, partly by necessity, and partly by unconscious accident, humanity is creating a pluralistic model of social organisation based on three organised sectors – government, for-profit and non-profit – operating in the context of an informal sector. Chart 1 opposite gives a diagrammatic expression of this idea, and much of this book is about where the three formal sectors intersect, that is the area where a great deal of my working life has been spent. It is as if the people of the world have an intuition that to get all their needs and aspirations met, they need the three organised sectors to make their individual contribution to the social whole, and then collaborate to promote maximum impact.

CHART 1

The Three Formal Sectors of a Modern Society

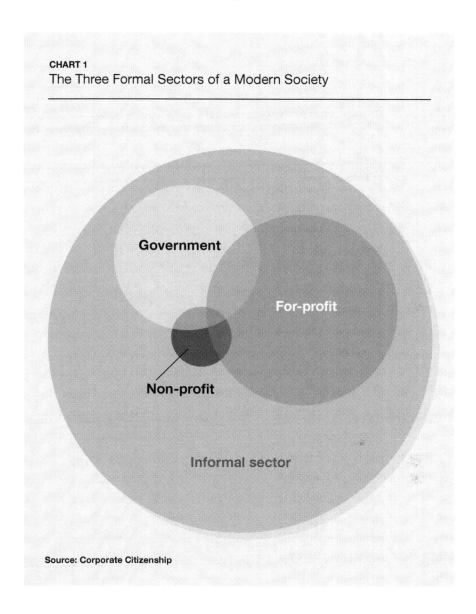

Source: Corporate Citizenship

The relative size of the three formal sector circles in Chart 1 will vary widely from society to society, both in terms of a share of national GDP and employment. For example, government expenditure as a share of GDP is 53.2% in Sweden, 45.1% in the UK, 39% in the USA and 29.3% in China.[36] In terms of employment, the public sector provides 29.2% of jobs in Sweden while the private sector provides about 70.8% and there is no good data for the non-profit sector. In Brazil only 12% of jobs are in the public sector and about 87% in the private sector.[37]

However, as a general trend over the past 30-plus years, the role of the state has contracted in society, and both the for-profit and the non-profit sectors have grown to fill the space that has been created. In parallel with the growth of the for-profit sector, the world has seen an unprecedented growth in independent non-profits working primarily, but not exclusively, to meet a wide range of humanity's social needs and environmental concerns. Consequently, we are seeing the creation of a good deal of commonality in humanity's social system, irrespective of the cultural difference that exists between nations and societies. The institutions of the three formal sectors are developing all around the world to meet different aspects of society's needs and wants.

The Rise of the Non-Profit Sector

The growth of independent non-profits and campaigning groups around the world is in many ways as important as the growth of private businesses. Both the communists and the fascists firmly suppressed any sort of independent citizens' group and subsumed social organisations like youth groups under state control; the communists had the Young Pioneers while the Nazis had the Hitler Youth. Independent non-profits and campaigning groups in particular represented an alternative centre of thought and action in society, and as a result they were totally unacceptable to totalitarian regimes.

While small in size compared with private firms (Walmart, the largest company in the Fortune Global 500, has revenues of $485.9bn and only about five non-profits in the USA have revenues of more than $1bn), non-profit organisations, like private firms, have grown rapidly in size and number over the past 40 years or so. Both types of organisation have benefitted immensely from the great economic, political and social changes that have gone on.

In historical terms, the non-profit sector has existed for millennia, but the first modern campaigning group emerged in Britain in the late 18th century, and was focused on the role of British business promoting the slave trade overseas. This was at a time when the British East India Company was at the height of its power and Britain was a 'proto-democracy', with a franchise limited to a small group of men with wealth. It was then that a group of Quakers (excluded from Parliament by the Test Acts) and Evangelical Christians came together to campaign to end the slave trade. Adam Hochschild tells the story of this campaign in his remarkable book *Bury the Chains*[38], and says it was perhaps the first time in history that a group of informed citizens came together to lobby their Parliament to introduce laws to forbid a business practise they considered reprehensible, and assert a new idea of morality.

In doing so, Hochschild says that these early campaigners pretty much invented all the tactics of lobbying and public campaigning that NGOs and non-profits take for granted and use today. They raised petitions, organised public rallies, created powerful visual media, canvassed support from MPs and their wives, and used direct mail fundraising. They also endorsed sugar and other products that had not been produced by slave labour, a precursor of the Fair Trade movement of today and generally created the template of campaigning which non-profits and charities have used ever since.

Having been founded in 1787, the campaign committee had so changed the moral climate in Britain, that in 1807 the Atlantic slave trade was formally abolished, and by 1833 the status of slavery was abolished throughout the British Empire. Here was an early and classic example of an independent voluntary organisation in a semi-democratic society holding both corporate interests and the state to account, and forcing a change in a policy that was a gross attack on the human rights of millions of Africans. In doing so, the campaigners also expanded the idea of democracy beyond the ballot box and Parliament, by giving ordinary citizens the ability to directly influence government. This type of activity is now found around the world and is growing in strength, utilising social media and the internet, and is rapidly reshaping many societies, including China's.

When a totalitarian state or an absolutist monarchy, such as Saudi Arabia, grants private citizens the space to engage in independent economic or social activity, they are diluting their control over society. It is in these spaces that citizens learn, in small and large businesses and charitable organisations, the skills of institutional management. While China has permitted and encouraged the growth of private economic activity and private firms, it has yet to give full legal recognition to independent non-profit social organisations. Nevertheless, they exist alongside state-sponsored social organisations because the people want and need them, and consequently, they have come together to create them.

As the world has opened up to a global economy and multinationals are found everywhere, so it is that Western non-profits such as Amnesty International, Oxfam, Médecins Sans Frontières, Care International and Save the Children have begun to work around the world too, even in former communist countries. They are also multinational institutions and they bring with them a critical attitude to many aspects of the behaviour of the government and private business. They perform an essential role in our new global system by questioning how society and the economy work for the common good. In my view, we cannot have healthy public and private sectors without a free press and a vigorous independent voluntary sector. Together they help to keep the other formal sectors honest and morally healthy.

This is not to say that non-profit organisations and campaigning groups are perfect – far from it. The recent scandal to touch a range of local and international aid agencies where there are serious allegations of staff being involved in exploitative relations with children is an unfortunate example.[39] Personally, I have only known two men go to jail for rank corruption, and they were both in the non-profit sector (the heads of New Era Philanthropy[40] and the United Way[41] in the USA). Non-profits, charities and religious bodies may have high moral aspirations, but they are human institutions after all. Just like companies and state bodies, they get things wrong and need to be confronted about their behaviour.

Not enough attention has been paid to the development of the non-profit 'civil society' sector around the world. It is often very local and grassroots in nature, and consequently hard to measure. In addition, the financial resources at the disposal of the voluntary non-profit sector are small compared with government and business, which can make it look weak. But its strength is measured in other ways: in its moral force based on public trust, its volunteers and active public support. When the public are asked to indicate what brands they most trust and non-profits like Amnesty

International and Oxfam are included, these organisations significantly lead over most commercial brands.

The Johns Hopkins Center for Civil Society Studies is one of the few examples of a sustained effort to understand how this sector is developing around the world. In 1997 Lester M. Salamon and Helmut K. Anheier began the process by publishing *Defining the Non-Profit Sector: A Cross-National Analysis*.[42] It began by seeking to define the sector and how it was developing in countries as diverse as France, Japan and the USA as well as in developing countries such as Brazil, India and Ghana. Unfortunately, there was only one study of the sector in the post-socialist world, which was Hungary. Subsequent publications by the Center have done much to flesh out our understanding of the size and focus of the sector along with its various sources of funding around the world, but there is much more work to be done to develop our understanding of the development of this sector.

A great change has been going on since the 1970s in how ordinary people seek to bring about change in society. When I was a member of the Labour Party in the 1970s and we were seeking to bring about change through the capture of state power at the ballot box, we had about eight times the members of the Royal Society for the Protection of Birds (RSPB), one relatively modest environmental non-profit. By the mid-2000s the RSPB had more members than all of the mainstream British political parties combined, and it has influenced both public policy and private companies to promote the protection of birds.

With the election of the socialist, leftist Jeremy Corbyn to the leadership of the Labour Party, there has been a new surge in members, which according the House of Commons Library in May 2018, now number 552,000. However, even with that figure combined with all other major parties, that still only gives 965,000 people in political party membership, whereas the RSPB still has over a million. I am no longer a member of the Labour Party but I am a member of the RSPB.

It is not just in Britain and the developed world that this trend for ordinary citizens to engage in social and environmental action thorough support for non-profits and NGOs is developing. There has been a surge in environmental non-profits in Asia and the Global Journal estimates that there are about 3 million non-profits in India alone engaging with a wide range of social, economic and environmental issues. The Philippines and Bangladesh, the home of the Grameen Bank and related organisations, both have vigorous non-profit sectors which have an impact on government and public policy as well as on the activities of the for-profits sector. In the USA, there are at least 1.4 million non-profits employing over 11 million people and being supported by many more volunteers and donors, and it, and the religious bodies that are part of it, are a major force in shaping national life.

The American Model?

The emerging global social model described here will seem normal to American readers because it is the one that the USA has lived with since its earliest days. The USA is one of the few countries in the world where the central government has never had an overtly socialist agenda, particularly if you ignore President Roosevelt's New Deal years. Its economic development has always relied on the for-profit sector, while social development initially relied on citizen action in the non-profit and informal sectors with individual states taking up social agendas such as education, particularly as the Federal Government is a relative newcomer to legislating for, and providing funding for, social initiatives.

To say this new global model is 'the American Model' is tempting but not true. Elements of it have been seen in many societies throughout history. Indeed, the early Mesopotamians had something resembling this model with private firms, temple charities and the state, all existing side by side, and each fulfilling different roles in society. In the Muslim world and across Asia there is clear evidence of citizen action and charitable work helping to build and unify societies. However, the USA, which borrowed key ideas and legal structures from Britain, has brought the model to its highest level of effectiveness in the modern world.

This is in part because within the idea of 'Americanism', the Federal Government, and the state sector in general, are a relatively small presence in society compared to many other countries. In 2015, the public sector was employing about 12% of the country's 121,490,000 workers. The US non-profit sector is correspondingly large and well organised, employing about 7%, while the rest of the workforce accounts for about 80% of the total who are in the private sector.[43] It is the for-profit sector which holds the greatest influence on society, but that is not the case in other parts of the world.

The USA has always relied on private firms to create its wealth and provide the goods and services it needs. It has been helped by having access to abundant raw materials and, in response, the creativity of the private sector has been immense. In the 19th and 20th centuries it was creating railroads, oil fields, housing, cars and a vast array of consumer goods. While there were many issues about the behaviour of private companies, they led the rising tide of prosperity. Today, that creativity can be seen at work in Silicon Valley, which has created firms such as Microsoft, Facebook and Google, and a whole range of technological wonders that form our digital and socially networked age.

Having such a dominant position in society from the early years of American independence, the for-profit sector and its leadership, including Andrew Carnegie, J.P. Morgan, the Rockefeller and Ford families, came to accept a responsibility to foster the non-profit sector as their contribution to the development of the country. The USA was, after all, a developing country in the days of Andrew Carnegie and this is all too easily forgotten. The model of social engagement that business chose to express its social responsibility was that of philanthropy, one of giving wealth created by business activity. This distinctly American model continues today in the work of Microsoft's Bill Gates, CNN's Ted Turner, Warren Buffet and many tech billionaires, although they now include the world beyond the USA in their philanthropic work.

Enlightened capitalists did exist outside of the US and Britain. They grew in many countries as the modern free market economy spread around the world. They sought to set standards of good behaviour in their business practices and support social development through major charitable donations and other good works. In Europe, the German Bosch and Daimler companies and Olivetti in Italy; the Tata family in India; and in South Eastern Asia, Cheong Fatt Tze, known as the Chinese Rockefeller, all followed this approach. However, they were exceptional people and during the socialist years their example has been written out of history almost as an anomaly in the capitalist system, a view many still hold.

While the model of a society based on three formal sectors is now found pretty much everywhere around the world, the size of the three formal sectors will vary greatly from country to country depending on levels of development, history, politics and other cultural factors. What is new is that the contraction of government as the dominant force in society has allowed the other two formal sectors to develop, and their very existence is important to shaping our planet's future. A social democratic country such as Sweden will always have a larger state sector than the USA, for example. While in a developing country like Brazil, around 11% to 12% of formal sector workers are in the public sector and 87% are in the private sector, but it seems that the non-profit voluntary sector employs about 2% to 3% of formal sector workers directly, but volunteers add another 3.7% to that total.[44]

As Chart 1 above shows, government and the two other emergent formal sectors, operate within the context of the informal sector, and more is said about this sector in the next chapter. But like government, it is a constant presence in society. It has spawned many political movements, small businesses and social protests over time. In developing countries in particular, the informal sector is massive. In South Asia it is estimated that about 75% of the population is in the informal sector. In other areas, such as Africa, it is even higher.

It is within this global social context that companies must now operate pretty much everywhere around the world, and while the changes between the roles of the formal sectors of society have raised many issues for private companies, there are other global developments of significance to be taken into account as well when we consider the importance of corporate citizenship. Some are internal to the for-profit sector, while others have developed in the wider social and political context of the world.

The existence of campaigning non-profits is only one factor pushing companies towards a greater sense of their wider role in the world and the need for good citizenship. There are many others but three stand out. One is internal to the modern company, where the growth of stakeholder theory has expanded the idea of the responsibilities of the company beyond those owed purely to its owners, the shareholders.

Two, since the founding of the United Nations, there is the steady development of a set of globally agreed values and rules in relation to both human life and the environment of the planet. Three, is an unprecedented global connectivity between people around the globe, where a bad accident in a supplier factory in the middle of Africa can be on the front page of *The Times* of London the next day. Each of these trends is examined below.

The Emergence of Stakeholder Theory

While there have been radical changes in economic and social structures in the new global society in the post-war years, there have also been developments in thinking about the company's role in society. While the legal situation for most Western companies is that they are still wholly owned by, and are accountable to, the shareholders – irrespective of how little time the shares have been held – the development of 'stakeholder theory' has mitigated that power and given prominence to the interest of others that have a 'stake' if not a share, in the business.

Stakeholder theory emerged in part as a reaction to the traditional assertion that the main purpose of business was to serve the interests of shareholders and maximise returns. More liberal business thinkers and others argued that while employees, suppliers, communities and more did not have shares in the business, they did have an important 'stake' in the business because its decisions could significantly affect their lives. For example, a worker might lose a job, suppliers a contract, and the community a source of employment and taxes. In addition, customers and consumers could face price rises and other changes that could be to their disadvantage. In a free market situation, the company needs a good reputation, and at the core of that reputation is what these stakeholders think of it. Consequently, company relations with stakeholders needs to be managed with care.

In the past 40 years or so, the interests of these human stakeholder groups have been joined by a consideration for the natural environment, and it is now included as a 'stakeholder' in business activities. The reasons behind adding the environment as a stakeholder vary. For some, it is a 'spiritual' consideration, a duty of care for the planet and other species in the same way that companies have a care for the people whose lives they touch. For others, it is a pragmatic awareness that serious damage to the planet's climate, oceans and biosphere will undoubtedly impair human life and be bad for business. From the days of the early coal mines and steel mills, it was obvious that business could have a major negative impact on a local environment, but from the late 1970s and 1980s it became obvious that business activity could also detrimentally affect the global environment.

Rachel Carson was one of the first people to highlight this issue with the publication in 1962 of *Silent Spring*,[45] which brought to the world's attention the effect of the indiscriminate use of pesticides on the environment. When the existence of large data sets about the impact of CFCs and carbon accumulation in the atmosphere became public in the 1970s, the global environmental impact of business became a serious consideration. Social and economic issues had always been a central part of considering business behaviour towards human stakeholders, but now we had added environmental concerns too. If all the people of China, India and Africa were to consume company products and services at the level of the average American or European, the world will be ravaged beyond repair and life itself difficult to sustain.

Because the social, political and environmental context for business has been changing rapidly at a local and global level, stakeholder theory is a very important contribution to helping companies respond, particularly as the definition of a stakeholder has now taken on a global aspect. And as supply and distribution chains have spread around the world, companies have broadened their sense of responsibility to include poor producers in the developing world, and to accept that poor consumers in developing countries need to be treated equally with wealthy ones in the West.

These concepts take the discussion of corporate responsibility well beyond the idea that companies are only responsible to shareholders as owners. While this remains legally true, there is a growing willingness for companies to accept a wider definition of their responsibilities. In the UK, company law has even been updated to require directors to 'have regard to the interests of employees' and 'consider the impact on the community and environment'. This is an acknowledgement of stakeholder theory and a step towards seeing the company as a corporate citizen with broadly based responsibilities as well as rights.

The Emergence of Global Values

Leaving aside the ideological and other conflicts of the post-war years, governments have been steadily fostering a vision of universal human rights that sets a radical new context for business operations. In 1947, with the creation of the UN and the issuing of the Universal Declaration of Human Rights,[46] governments decisively changed the global context for business activity. The Universal Declaration clearly said that slavery was wrong, child labour was wrong, people had the right to a fair trial, women and men shared a basic equality, people had the right to own property and much more.

The Universal Declaration, and subsequent conventions derived from it, have begun to set out for both governments, businesses, non-profits and individuals, what is owed as a right to every person around the world. Whatever else people and nations disagreed on, governments were prepared to commit to some basic statements of values about the human condition, and in doing so have begun to create a new ethical and, on occasion, legal context for global society.

As government's control of national economies and enterprises has declined and private sector firms re-emerged to take leadership of the global economy, they have done so within a global framework of values, laws and regulations about human relations and environmental responsibilities, that would have been a total mystery to the East India Company. Today, while governments around the world have given more space in society for business to operate, they have also helped create a framework of values, ideas and laws that guide its actions worldwide. National laws remain important, as do those of trading blocs such as the EU, but we now have, at the global level, a framework of values and laws to constrain and guide human and business behaviour. The Universal Declaration also enjoins all organs of society to pay regard to its statements and to work to implement them. This includes business and the millions of private companies around the world.

It has to be acknowledged that the system is imperfect, and the Universal Declaration itself probably needs updating, but the trend to create global values and standards based on an understanding of the value of human life, is now firmly established. This is shown by the creation of the UN

Global Compact for businesses, and the recent publication by the UN of Global Sustainable Development Goals (SDGs).[47] The SDGs were in part developed with business consultation, and they are the latest step in changing the moral climate about companies' business responsibilities in the world.

While many companies are lobbying internationally on the basis of their self-interest in trade and corporate tax laws, for example, the wider society through the SDGs and other means, has begun to create a more comprehensive framework of global values in which business should be conducted. Particularly through the work of the UN, the world has begun to prepare the ground for a global economy, by articulating the values on which it should be based. While more remains to be done, the process of shaping a global sense of responsibility for humanity and the physical environment continues to move forward, irrespective of political and economic conflicts between nation states and trading blocs.

The key question for the future is: what do each of the three organised sectors bring to this process of creating and maintaining global standards of behaviour? Above all, how should companies, as the drivers of the global economy, be responding? In order to understand the different, sometimes conflicting and sometimes collaborating roles that the three organised sectors play in the process of building our common future, we need to know more about them individually, and that issue is addressed in the next two chapters.

Global Interconnectedness

It is private companies that have in the past and today do so much to promote the interconnectedness of the world. Trade, foreign investment, global sourcing and cheap foreign travel have enabled so many people to expand their horizons beyond national boundaries. However, since the invention of the internet and the mass marketing of personal computers and mobile phones linked to the world wide web, we have seen an explosion in global connectedness. This has worked to great advantage for businesses large and small, as they have been able to expand their business activities on a worldwide basis. New consumers and customers, sources of raw materials and low-cost suppliers can now be found at the click of a mouse.

The ordinary citizen has also been empowered by the new technology of our age in an unprecedented way. They can compare the market like never before and search for products and services from around the world at the lowest price or best value. They can speak to family and friends on the other side of the planet, and they can make their views known about issues that concern them. For companies husbanding their reputations with care, this is a massive development. Customers and consumers want their companies, their brand names in particular, to have high standards and they don't want to be eating chocolate or wearing clothes produced by child labour or in a sweatshop. There is a growing global sense of the equality of human life, its value worldwide and fears for the environment that sustains it. Modern media is giving a vital expression to those concerns.

One of my earliest experiences of this development was in 1996 working for the British retailer Marks & Spencer on its first supplier code. This was a company with a long and well-respected record of social responsibility and good treatment of its workers. It could proclaim as late as the 1970s that nearly all the products sold in its stores in Britain were sourced from Britain, and that it proudly supported British industry. It doesn't make that claim now. In the 1980s and 1990s it had started to contract with suppliers overseas and was soon embroiled, through a TV programme produced by *World in Action* in January 1996, in a scandal over the use of child labour and other issues in a Moroccan supplier factory.[48]

The company took the programme makers to court and won a libel case, but shortly afterwards published its first ever supplier code. Previously, its merchandisers would visit UK factories regularly and the British suppliers knew what was expected of them in terms of social responsibility and issues like child labour. However, with a global supply chain, personal contact and mutual understanding between the company and its suppliers was more difficult, and it became clear it needed to be formalised. The company needed to set out its values in writing and publish a clear statement of responsible behaviour to guide its new foreign suppliers.

Today, the TV programme would be replaced by a campaigning non-profit taking photos on a mobile phone. Or, as in the case of the international environmental organisation Greenpeace in 2010, it was able to support its campaign against deforestation by palm oil companies in Borneo, by showing changes in the landscape by using Google Maps as evidence for its claims.[49] At that time, I was working for Golden Agri, Indonesia's largest palm oil producer and seeking to respond to the case that Greenpeace was mounting. It did successfully respond to the challenge, in part because, from the onset of the Greenpeace campaign, it took the view that while its business was overwhelmingly focused on Asia, it was part of a globally interconnected world and it aspired to have global standards which could be transparently enforced and that modern technology left no hiding place for those wanting to cheat on them.

CHAPTER 4:

The World Companies Now Live in

Today's Mix of Social Sectors

A global pattern of governmental, for-profit and non-profit sectors operating within the context of an informal sector is rapidly becoming the global norm. Each of the formal sectors has special capacities and skills, and human beings want to benefit from the activities of all three. While our media is full of conflicts between nation states, political alliances, trading blocs, social and religious groups, there is, beneath the surface, a steady pattern of development around the world based on the three formal sectors. This is the world companies increasingly live in and it has profound implications for their sense of citizenship in a modern global society.

If there is to be any hope of gaining full advantage from this recent development, active corporate engagement with the other two formal sectors is vital. If the for-profit sector just looks after its own interests, which is something it is prone to do, who looks after the social whole? Companies will make a contribution to society through their business activities, but they cannot abandon its wider development to the leadership of governments and the non-profit sectors. Companies need to be able to play a constructive role with both of the other two sectors and interact positively with the informal sector around the great issues of our time.

Consequently, it is important for companies to understand their relationship as citizens, with the other two formal sectors, and the potential of their own role within the informal sector. Understanding the different roles and capacities of the other sectors and how they work within society as a whole, is critical to developing the wider role of the company in society. Yet again, the relative size and nature of the three sectors will vary from society to society for reasons of history, culture and politics, but that doesn't matter much. A modern society needs all three to operate well as individual components and to collaborate effectively on critical issues. What matters is that the principle is established, that each of the 'social partners' has a role to play in shaping society for the common good.

Companies are living in a new world and need to embrace the opportunities it offers, not just when doing business, but to be an active corporate citizen. Therefore, they need to know much more about their potential partners, and not just from the point of view of the company's self-interest. That is important and legitimate, but good citizenship is about going beyond a narrowly defined self-interest and is about reaching out to play a wider role in society for the common good. This chapter briefly identifies what each brings to the table, picking up points of connection for companies between all four sectors of society.

Global Companies in the Global System

While companies come in all shapes and sizes and very many of them are purely local or national in character, it is the large international companies that are creating the global economy and linking societies together. They have done it in the past, but today the speed and scale of their operations is unprecedented. One of the best guides to their scale and activities is the Fortune Magazine Global 500 list of companies. In the 2017 issue, the top 500 companies of the world had $27.7tr in sales, generated $1.5tr in profits and employed 67 million people directly. These multinational companies have integrated business systems that span the globe and are huge in cash terms. Their sheer size and economic importance alone, means that their commitment to good corporate citizenship is potentially a vital contribution to our global society.

When compared with countries, a company's Cash Value Added (CVA) is reasonably comparable to a country's GDP. In the case of Unilever, ranked only 140th in the 2017 Fortune Global 500, its CVA is 15 billion Euro a year. That makes it roughly the same size as Jamaica in cash terms, which has a GDP of $14.9bn. Therefore Unilever, in cash terms, is larger than 71 of the world's other countries smaller than Jamaica (the exchange rate in 2017 was on average 1.1 Euro to a US Dollar). In addition, it is estimated that the company provides for almost one billion consumers a week around the world and millions of people are dependent on it for their livelihoods.[50]

In a 2005 study of its business in Indonesia, undertaken jointly with Oxfam, it was estimated that the 7,069 full-time jobs in Unilever's Indonesia operations created approximately 290,000 full-time equivalent jobs in the company's value chain of backward and forward linkages to the local economy.[51] Jamaica's population in 2017 was just over 2.8 million.

In the post-war years and at the height of the Cold War, US-based companies dominated multinationals. They had come out of the Second World War having done very well. Their production capacity was immense and competition from the Japanese and Germans was non-existent, while the British, French and other countries in Europe were virtually bankrupt – if the companies had not been sold off to pay for the war, they were exhausted by it. In the 1960s, the phrase 'Coca-Cola imperialism' was common as the US dominated the listings of the world's largest companies but even by 2010, US multinationals only accounted for 30% of the top 500 global multinationals. With a resurgent Europe having 35%, developed Asia (eg Japan and Korea) having 20%, the remaining 74 companies came from developing and emerging economies.

This trend towards the 'democratisation' of the Fortune Global 500 has continued until today, such that in 2017, the USA's Walmart was still the largest company on the list. As the dollar value of the sales of Exxon and other oil companies in particular have declined, the next three largest companies on the list are Chinese. In 2017, China had 109 companies or 22% of Global 500 listings of the largest companies.[52]

The relationship between Russian and Chinese multinationals and their home country governments remains much closer that that between Western companies and their home country governments. Multinationals can still be used as instruments of state power even if they are nominally independent institutions, and it remains to be seen how these vast new companies from former communist countries behave in the global marketplace.

A complicating factor is that investment has globalised too, and while a company may be French, Swiss, Indian, Chinese or Argentinean by country of origin and culture, their shareholders and customers could be anywhere in the world, so to which stakeholder do they owe a loyalty? As the aging societies of the West have looked to bolster their pension funds, they have been more than happy to invest in any number of rapidly growing companies around the world. So, while a company might be Indian by origin, it may well have many foreign 'owners' in the form of shareholders based overseas.

Nevertheless, while international and other companies around the world have a lot in common, they are still influenced by their culture of origin. In books like *The Seven Cultures of Capitalism*, and *Varieties of Capitalism*[53], scholars are starting to show how national culture and public policy influences the business culture of companies and even their comparative advantage. However, the book now needs to take into account massive companies originating in China, Russia, Brazil and other parts of the developing world. How do they see their role in society? What are the stakeholders they recognise and where do their ultimate loyalties lie? Are they just an international extension of the home state's power in a new form, or do they have an independent culture of their own?

Fortune Magazine ranks companies by their sales but if they were ranked by foreign assets then the global pattern would look somewhat different. Western Companies would be dominating because they have been investing overseas for so much longer than the Chinese. Shell, for example, has about 74% of its workers overseas. In order for it and other multinationals to manage their citizenship both at home and around the world, they need to have a detailed knowledge of their total economic, social and environmental footprint, not only in terms of direct employees, but also in terms of the forward and backward linkages of the business to society.

Only a few Western companies have published information about this. The true scale of their interaction with society on a global basis is still largely unknown. SABMiller, Coca-Cola, Unilever and Diageo are among the small number of companies that have, to some degree, attempted this type of economic and social impact-mapping; they have published reports on a country by country basis that give some real insight into the type of impact they have locally, and that information is extremely useful to potential partners and others in society.

It is not just in supply chain, production and distribution that companies exert influence through creating jobs, it is also through their products and what they offer consumers around the world. The explosion in the use of computers and mobile phones is just one indicator of how global companies are changing our lives; they, not governments, are the ones spreading the use of the handheld technology and internet use around the world. Vodafone's publications on the impact of mobile phones in Africa, for example, are really informative both in terms of macro-economics but also in terms of the impact they have on the lives of ordinary people. Today, a retailer based in London can take baby sweetcorn picked in Kenya, wash it and bag it with the correct barcode and have it on the shelves of a supermarket within 48 hours. That is the power of companies to achieve global integration of our food supply chain and change people's lives at both ends of the value chain.

Government

First among the two formal sectors by size and practical importance from a company's point of view is the governmental sector. It licenses companies and their business activities, creates the framework of law in which they operate, regulates and taxes them. It also has a big interest in the social responsibility of its corporate citizens. Governments all around the world have huge economic, social and environmental agendas that can often only be achieved with the engagement and co-operation of private companies. Governments can legislate, levy taxes, give tax incentives or try to shame companies into doing things they see as important, but they know that many of the problems they face depend on private firms to help in their resolution. How to work with them then becomes an important issue for governments of all types.

Despite the general trend in recent years to reduce the power of government in society, and in some countries in particular, it still remains immense. On the other hand, where governments are weak, as seen in some developing countries, private companies will take on and solve social problems for their workers such as health, housing and education to ensure that business can go on. They have in the past created corporate welfare states to make sure they have healthy and productive workers. They have even taken on security as an issue. The East India Company had its own navy and army and even today in Africa and other parts of the world, a major section of the workforce of oil companies is made up of armed guards.

But, if the government of a country such as North Korea says 'no' to private business, then there will be none, and likewise charities and social organisations. Government grants the licence to operate, a key phrase in the argument about why companies should be good citizens, especially for oil and other companies closely controlled by governments.

The mandate of modern government in most case does not just rest on the power of coercion, there is a large component of practical utility in the legitimacy of a government; the people need to prosper and feel secure as a result of its policies and practices. Consequently, many forms of government have co-opted or simply allowed the for-profit sector to function because it provides the people with what they want and need, as well as being a good source of taxes.

Perhaps for this reason, private companies have been allowed to flourish under totalitarian governments, but then what is good corporate citizenship? Companies do have a certain degree of independent power in society and they can on occasion soften the diktats of government, if not overturn them completely. For example, in my working life, I have known Levi's to bring African American workers into their factories in Southern States that operated a complete colour bar in the 1950s, I have seen Unilever find a way to bring women in to the workplace in Saudi Arabia and seen other Western companies give workers in China some freedom of expression beyond the state-managed trade unions, so it is not all a one-way street.[54]

Precisely because the state does retain tremendous power over businesses and the marketplace generally, businesses are very interested in politics and undertake much lobbying to promote their self-interest. This is often through trade associations. Corporate lobbying is the source of much concern to many non-profits dealing with issues such as carbon emissions, tax reform and advertising to children. Much of what the for-profit sector does is not overtly political, consequently, politicians and leaders of many political persuasions feel able to live with it. That is until issues such as the price of energy, rail travel, sugar and salt levels in food or plastic packaging become of public concern. Then an everyday business activity becomes 'political' and often 'the people' or their non-profit spokespersons demand government action to remedy the situation.

Governments can, and will, intervene to correct wrongs and change company practices if they see fit. As noted in the previous chapter, despite intense counter lobbying from business interests, the British government acted in 1806 to ban the slave trade. Laws were passed to constrain British registered ships from engaging in the slave trade but not all obeyed the new law. Furthermore, nothing happened beyond British legal jurisdiction. The trade was an international problem, not just one affecting British businesses. As Sian Rees shows in her book *Sweet Water and Bitter*,[55] it took 60 years of armed interventions by Britain in Africa, on the high seas, with diplomatic and military action against countries such as Spain, Portugal, Brazil and the USA, to bring the Atlantic slave trade to a final conclusion. The law is a powerful tool for regulating business. But even today, and despite many international agreements and a growing body of international law, it tends to be limited to a national jurisdiction.

It is not the activities of international companies such as Coca-Cola in a country like Sweden that gets public attention. Sweden is a democracy, with the rule of law, a free press and active citizen organisations scrutinising both government and the private sector. It is in poor and developing countries where the framework of law is weak, enforcement poor, corruption rife and the citizen's voice hard to hear. It is in these countries that the behaviour of business comes under scrutiny – just as it did with respect to the slave trade. In poor countries where governments are weak, there is space for companies to adopt lower standards of behaviour on issues like child labour that would not be acceptable in the home country. Ikea, for example, has gone to great lengths to assure customers and Swedish regulators that its hand-woven rugs sourced from South East Asia are ethically sourced, without the use of child labour, a practice that has been normal in several industries in that part of the world.

In poor countries in particular, there is also space for companies to shape government policy through grand corruption and bribery not much seen in the Western world these days. Government controls access to raw materials and markets within its jurisdiction, and there are many cases of politicians being willing to sell that access for a bribe, and many businesses have taken advantage of that opportunity.

In one month alone in April 2018, three world leaders faced imprisonment for corruption involving companies and their owners. Park Geun-hye of South Korea, Luiz Inacio Lula da Silva of Brazil and Jacob Zuma of South Africa all fell from grace because of their corrupt relations with companies that should have known better. The companies involved could and should have refused to participate in the bribery and other corrupt practices involving these heads of state, but they didn't. Some hoped to gain from it, others felt they would suffer if they didn't do what was asked by Park Geun-hye, for example. As a result, they tarnished their reputation, compromised their democracy and undermined the public's faith in their social system.

The pressure is on against this type of corruption and companies need to choose which side they are on. If a company is going to suffer, it is best that it is done in a good cause rather than compromise themselves. Companies need good government and effective regulation to be able to do business efficiently and effectively; they have a vested interest in honest effective public governance. Bribes cost money and represent huge reputational, legal and financial risks from fines, as the US Foreign Corrupt Practices Act makes clear.[56] One of the first prosecutions after the passing of the act in 1977 was of Chiquita Brands for bribing the President of Honduras over taxes, and since that time the OECD has introduced an anti-bribery Code and the British Government has brought in the 2010 Bribery Act.

There are huge spaces between country governments and while these are often filled by treaties and international agreements, international companies are truly global in their thinking. They can and do make business decisions to protect the economic interests of the business as a whole irrespective of national interests. They have real choices about where they will invest and what countries they will do business in, and today these choices are worldwide. While businesses have many agendas with governments – typically lower taxes and less legislation – their primary 'political' agenda down the ages has been the free movement of goods, the free movement of capital and the free movement of labour. These are all very much in the interest of businesses as 'rational' economic institutions, but these demands have profound implications for the economy and culture of different societies around the world.

A world based on such a totally free trade agenda seems as unlikely as one based on world communism. The social and economic consequences are too difficult for diverse societies to deal with in the compressed timescales of today. The Brexit vote in Britain and the election of President Trump in the USA seems to show people reacting against the globalisation trend led by international business following its self-interest. If leaders from the UK and the USA cannot handle the economic and social impacts of a free trade agenda, having done so much to promote it throughout history, then what can other governments do? Consequently, many countries today are looking for a more pragmatic approach that accepts the private sector has a role in society and are looking for ways of engaging it as a corporate citizen in addressing the many issues they face.

Companies are active players in shaping public policy and seeking to do so in their own economic self-interest, but what about the public interest? Can they also develop a view on issues that are beyond their immediate economic self-interest and act on them? There is some evidence that they can, but that requires having values that transcend the purely economic and bottom line mission of the company. Do companies just do what they are told or do they have the character and capacity to make a stand for what they think is right? On issues like climate change, plastic waste and sexual identity rights, which may not be covered fully by law, does a company just wait for government action or does it have the capacity within its own organisation to develop a view that fits with its experience of the world? These are key questions for business today. Defining its place in society may depend on the answer.

Keeping the law is generally part of good corporate citizenship, but so is reaching out voluntarily to address key problems in society by adjusting business practices and contributing to community initiatives. Private firms are so often the obvious partners for governments to work with on critical issues but both parties need to have the will and capacity to engage. That requires companies to have the vison and values to do so, and a clear sense of the agenda that fits with their own special identity. They cannot just respond to every political demand made on them by government, and it needs to know how best to mobilise corporate engagement in ways that make sense for the wider diversity of companies within its jurisdiction.

The Non-Profit Sector

The world's rapidly emerging non-profit sector, while small in resource terms compared with companies and government, is an increasingly vital part of global society. This organised sector has several names – the voluntary sector, the charity sector, non-governmental organisations (NGOs) – and spokespeople for the sector often like to call it 'civil society'. All are useful and meaningful names and in 1997, Lester M. Salamon and Helmut K. Anheier said:[57]

> "…we have come to accept the existence of two grand complexes of organisations – two broad sectors – into which it has become conventional to divide social life: the market and the state, or the private and public sectors.

> "…no such agreement prevails, however about the existence, let alone the precise contours, of a third complex of institutions, a definable 'third sector' occupying a distinctive social space outside of both the market and the state."

I have used their term non-profit as the descriptor of the sector, in part because it clearly distinguishes the sector from the for-profit sector, or as they call it, the 'private sector'. This sector does not exist to generate profits and is not guided by commercial goals. It is in essence that broad collection of citizen-created and led organisations that work on a wide range of economic, social and environmental issues. It is comprised of small voluntary local groups through to major charities that are run like large businesses. It also includes religious organisations, trade unions, mutual self-help groups, some co-ops and non-profit commercial enterprises, local and international campaigning groups, and many would argue, institutions like universities and the BBC.

It is a very broad-based and eclectic group, recognised in law as institutions with a mission to serve their members or the wider public – not a group of shareholders. While the profit motive is in theory absent, it does creep in with some organisations striving to increase the 'surplus' on their trading activities and charities do compete vigorously against each other for donations.

While some of the larger charities and organisations are comparable to small and medium businesses, the overall size of the sector, even in the USA where the non-profit sector is one of the most established, it probably does not exceed about 7% of GDP. However, it is growing rapidly around the world, and it does employ a lot of people. It draws revenues from fees and trading, philanthropy and government funding. Furthermore, it is supported by a wider number of volunteers who contribute their free time. In France, for example, the UN estimates that about 5.8% of the population work in the sector but that another 3.2 % of the workforce volunteer in support of its work; in Brazil those figures are 2% to 3% of the workforce being employed in the sector, supported by another 3.7% of the workforce volunteering to help.[58]

The non-profit sector has a long tradition of relying on charitable giving to support its activities, and the motive for these donations often began as part of many religious traditions. All of the great religions put a responsibility on those who have, to care for those who have not, and charitable giving has been the traditional way of individuals, and companies for that matter, to discharge that obligation. It is possible that the Mesopotamians had temples independent of the state that received gifts from individuals and businesses to honour the gods, provide for sacrifices and do good works in society. Certainly, the Greeks, Romans and early Christians did, as did many religious organisations in the Middle East and Asia.

The concept of charitable status and the creation of legally recognised charitable institutions was first fully codified in the English-speaking world by Queen Elizabeth I in an Act of Parliament in 1601,[59] which was about the time that the British East India Company was established. The preamble recognised the relief of poverty, education, support for religion and many other good works as being 'charitable purposes'. It recognised that money given for these reasons was money dedicated to God's purpose and that the state should not seek to tax or interfere with such gifts. Thus, a sense of independence from the state was established early in the tradition of these organisations and it continues today. Most recently updated in 2006, charities still have considerable tax relief for pursuing 'charitable purposes' but not overtly political ones.

In his two books, *American Exceptionalism: The Two Edged Sword* [60] and *Why it Never Happened Here: Why America Never Became Socialist,*[61] Seymour Martin Lipset says that American society was founded on the political principles of the Protestant sects such as the Presbyterians, Unitarians, Quakers and Baptists. They not only encouraged an ethic of economic self-reliance, self-help and approved of business, but each sect also acted to establish churches, schools, hospitals, libraries and other institutions to promote public wellbeing, honour God's injunction to read scripture, and do good works.

Their outlook was the foundation of the American social model, one based on a small Federal Government, a free market and private economic enterprise complemented by one of the world's most vigorous non-profit sectors. In its origins the Federal State did have a role in regulating the market and foreign trade in particular, as well as providing infrastructure and making some social provisions, but independent collective action by citizens was fostered as the frontline of the local social provisions of education, health and many other services in that vast country.

This is not just the experience of the English-speaking world. In the Muslim world there are clear instructions in the Qur'an for believers to give 2.4% of their assets to the poor each year. This voluntary 'zakat' is one of the five pillars of Islam and has led to a long tradition of setting up foundations or 'waqfs' to do good works in promoting the faith and for the public good, such as establishing and maintaining wells and schools. The Buddhist, Hindu and Jewish faiths, among others, have scripture that enjoins followers to act to promote the good of others, irrespective of what the state may be doing. That impulse continues today and from this common religious root we have many modern secular organisations, particularly in the environmental field, but also other community groups and social organisations.

Whatever the impulse that leads to their creation and activity, non-profits are very often citizen-created and citizen-led. The interests and commitment of private citizens drives the sector. Chart 2 opposite shows the source of funding for the non-profit sector in the USA, and it is the funds raised from ordinary citizens that are the major sources of support. The corporate contribution may be somewhat larger than stated because the Foundation's component includes corporate foundations, as well as private ones like the

Gates and Carnegie Foundations. This shows individual giving as by far the largest element (72%).

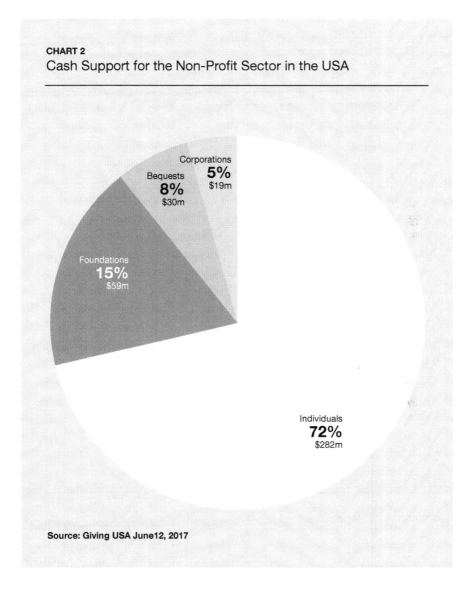

CHART 2
Cash Support for the Non-Profit Sector in the USA

Corporations
5%
$19m

Bequests
8%
$30m

Foundations
15%
$59m

Individuals
72%
$282m

Source: Giving USA June12, 2017

However, research from Johns Hopkins University shows that the pattern of this funding varies around the world and support from the corporate sector is a real but small part of the mix of non-profit funding, which often includes earned income from fees and trading.[62] Many non-profits, including some in the USA, also receive major and growing support from government. That is because governments can see the value of these organisations and, rather than provide services themselves, are willing to help fund non-profits to do the work on the ground.

In 2016/17 of Oxfam's total income of £408m, £178m came from government (43%), £108m from donations and legacies (26%), and £90.9m from trading sales (22%) and the rest from other sources, including in-kind giving.[63] Whether this type of 'sub-contracting' for the state will have a fundamental impact on the culture of the sector remains to be seen. However, it is perhaps indicative of the contraction of the state in the social sphere, as well as the economic one, and a recognition of the superior effectiveness of non-state actors in certain situations.

With their historical roots, the large majority of non-profits are in fact service providers; they are caring institutions. They work with people in many ways to help them face issues and otherwise improve their lives. The sector seeks to serve the people, often the neediest, and they do their work with the passion that comes from having a close connection with an urgent need and a strong desire to address it. At their best, these organisations are highly motivated and on a mission to change people's lives for the better, and as time has gone by, to protect animals and the environment generally. They are overwhelmingly focused on single groups or issues in society but by working with and on them, they change how society as a whole views and acts on many economic, social and environmental problems.

A good example would be the hospice movement in the UK, the first of which was founded by Dame Cicely Saunders in 1967 and it has now grown to become a worldwide movement and its lessons widely adopted, even in Africa.[64] Cicely Saunders worked in the government National Health Service and a voluntary sector hospice run by the Sisters of Charity before setting up her own hospice with voluntary support, to better manage the care of dying patients. She learned from the past and took the initiative to do something about a situation that concerned her and many others, blending her modern medical skills with a long tradition of compassionate care. In doing so, her example ultimately changed the National Health Service's own internal practices with regard to end-of-life care.

Some charities combine both direct service to people in need with active campaigning when the organisation feels it necessary. They have great credibility as a result of their frontline practical experience in war-torn and famine-ridden areas, for example. That experience, their concern for others and independence from political and business interests, allows them to speak bluntly to the power of governments, international agencies and companies when they see them failing people or other species and the environment generally. Oxfam, Save the Children, Care International and WWF are examples of such organisations that mix campaigning with providing care for people and the environment around the world irrespective of national boundaries. Companies will work with such groups on various issues but are also subject to their campaigning when the charities feel the need to criticise them.

When in 1787 a committee of Anglicans and Quakers formed the committee to abolish the slave trade, they expanded the idea of citizen voluntary action into the area of campaigning for social justice and set the template for the activities of many such organisations that have followed. Amnesty International is a good example. It is a purely campaigning group set up to fight for the human rights of individuals and groups around the world. It does not do 'service provision', as it is normally understood, even when it helps individuals in prison; all of its work is campaigning in one form or another. Amnesty in particular makes great use of the Universal Declaration of Human Rights and the many conventions associated with it in fighting the case for human rights around the world. It will use judicial processes where it can and campaigns to highlight some of the world's worst human rights abuses.

Greenpeace, however, will use direct action against governments and companies alike, when it sees the need. It confronted the French government over the testing of nuclear weapons in the Pacific, and also occupied the offices of Unilever in protest against its use of palm oil, which is associated with deforestation and threatens the existence of animals such as the orangutan in Indonesia. These non-profits, including Oxfam and Médecins Sans Frontières, take a global view of economic, social and environmental issues, and in that respect they are not unlike international companies.

Such campaigning groups take a high moral position on the issues that concern them and they are able to do that because they define their role as acting in the public good. They are financially and morally supported by large numbers of private individuals who recognise and value their judgments, because they are not compromised by political interests or the pursuit of profits.

They get the media attention because they are bold, vigorous and are often the first to identify emerging issues. Also, they develop high levels of expertise in their chosen issue areas because they have a tight focus of attention on specific topics, such as the human rights of indigenous peoples, the impact of plastic on marine life and oil pipelines on the migration of elk. This practical and scientific expertise also gives them great authority. Like universities, which can also be counted in this sector, they employ some extremely well qualified and thoughtful people, who have the time and passion for the great issues of our day. Companies are foolish to ignore their contribution and can learn a lot from it.

This tight focus on single issues is often a great strength for non-profits compared with governments and companies; they have to focus on many issues at a time. At other times, governments and companies may not identify social and environmental problems because they are the unintended consequences of a well-meaning policy or practice. It has already been said that this sector generally, and campaigning non-profits in particular, help keep the other two formal sectors honest by challenging them both philosophically and in practical terms, by creative forms of service provision and campaigning.

Where there is no free press or a reliable rule of law, they are a particularly vital part of society. They articulate and act on the people's needs and concerns, and so often are the leading edge of debate on the great issues of our time at home and abroad. They link up with sister organisations around the world, and many authoritarian governments are distinctly uncomfortable with the national non-profits having funding and links with agencies abroad. Several such governments are trying to restrict the activities of international non-profits in their jurisdiction.

The fact that non-profits will invest in thoughtful research is a key issue for international food companies, for example, because they do not have highly trained environmentalists on the ground in Borneo studying the wider social and environmental impacts of the palm oil industry. They are usually just buying the stuff in the marketplace from what seems a reliable supplier. It is Greenpeace, WWF and other non-profits that invest in such research, for example, studying the impact of modern fishing techniques on global fish stocks from the point of view of long-term sustainability. The food companies become the victim of their own tight focus on doing business as they see it today. They are following their traditional script, and often don't have the will or the management capacity to think about the long-term implications of their actions.

However, in recent years we have seen companies taking the initiative to join with non-profit organisations, and sometimes governments, in multi-stakeholder initiatives such as the Roundtable on Sustainable Palm Oil (RSPO), and the World Cocoa Foundation, which is supported by a number of companies. The sustainable fishing initiative, the Marine Stewardship Council, was launched jointly by Unilever and WWF in 1996 to address issues that the non-profit world was critical to identifying. This trend is very positive and is an example of the kind of future for business this book is arguing for.

This is not to say that the campaigning non-profits are always right. They are an important player in the process of how society comes to identify and understand issues, but deciding what to do about them is another matter. A good historic example of non-profits being badly wrong about a public policy response to a social problem was the campaign by the Anti-Saloon League and the Women's Christian Temperance Union among others, to close down the private companies producing alcohol in the USA. They were right in identifying that the irresponsible consumption of alcohol was part of many of America's social problems, such as poverty and family violence, but badly wrong in the solution they advocated.[65]

Following intensive lobbying of politicians in 1920, they managed to get the US government to ban the production and sale of alcohol in America. The country entered an era of prohibition for 13 years, but in 1934, and at the height of the depression, President Roosevelt overturned the ban – prohibition was just not working. The non-profit solution of abolition had created unforeseen social and economic problems and was depriving farmers of a major market and government of much needed taxes. Consequently, other citizen-based pressure groups grew up, seeking to overturn the ban. It is one thing to identify a problem, and another to prescribe the solution from the perspective of a single-issue pressure group. Moral certainty may drive single issue campaigns but it is not always the best guide to practical solutions in a complex world.

My personal experience of such campaigns includes working with Cadbury's on issues around cocoa sourcing from Ghana. The company helped set up the industry starting in Ghana in 1908, but in 1956 the post-independence government had taken an ever increasing role in managing the industry, and Cadbury's presence in the country was reduced to a staff of about two that bought cocoa from the government controlled Cocoa Board.

In 2001, Cadbury was still importing about 90% of its cocoa from Ghana, but public attention was focused on how chocolate was produced, following press reports of extensive child slavery in cocoa farms. The company reacted immediately and I was part of a team that went to Ghana to review the situation. In response, the company sought to re-engage with the farming community.[66] In 2009, it announced that it would source its cocoa in partnership with the Fairtrade Foundation, a non-profit that was campaigning to give farmers in the developing world a fair stable price for their product, along with extra payments that could be used to strengthen their business or the community.

It was an excellent idea with a strong moral foundation, but my concern at the time was essentially a practical one, as Fairtrade was then sourcing 500 tons of cocoa from Ghana whereas Cadbury was sourcing more in the region of 25,000 tons. Questions already existed about how an ethical purchasing policy could work in a fluctuating global marketplace for cocoa, but also could Fairtrade act at scale? Did this small non-profit have the capacity to deliver the degree of ethical control and social progress it promised? This was a concern because Cadbury had effectively transferred the problem of ethically monitoring small farmers in Ghana to the charity. By 2016, its new owners Mondelez International, were looking for solutions through its own company project Cocoa Life, which closely shadows the Fairtrade approach but is run by the company itself. The values of Fairtrade had been asserted, but the implementation was passed back to the company. The impact that will have on consumer perceptions has yet to be understood.

It is also highly probable that some company leaders and politicians resent being made to feel morally inferior by such campaigns, others resent the fact that they are not on top of the issues. Campaigning non-profits do like to present themselves as the innocent child who points out that the corporate and governmental 'emperors' have no clothes. However, business leaders have to get over that and learn to play their part in the debate about the big issues, so that we can devise workable solutions. It is the price they and we all pay for the freedom of a democracy; even if at times the non-profits can be seen as 'the boy who cries wolf' or 'the princess and the pea', because they are never satisfied with the improvements that are made.

Single issue pressure group politics can be difficult for companies and governments to cope with because some campaigning non-profits don't want to enter into dialogue. These organisations stand aside from the process of engagement that is suggested here. This does not disqualify them from the public debate. They have their reasons for doing what they do. Amnesty International is a prime example because it takes a strong moral stand on human rights issues and does not want to be drawn into a process of pragmatic negotiating around the issues. The solution for companies wanting engagement and expert advice on the issues was to help set up a new organisation called the Business & Human Rights Resource Centre, which develops the expertise and engages in dialogue with companies around an issue to find solutions to practical problems.

Lastly, it is worth saying that many members of this sector are often called non-governmental organisations or NGOs. This name was effectively coined by the UN, which as a club of governments was constantly being lobbied by a range of non-profits on issues as diverse as trade policy, refugees, heritage sites and migration. The UN needed a category into which these noisy lobbyists could be fitted and, since they were not government organisations, they were called 'non-governmental organisations' (NGOs) and the terms on which they had access to the UN were defined accordingly. They did initially have much more access to the UN than the big multinationals, which at the height of the Cold War were viewed with suspicion as exploitative, colonialist, capitalists. However, following the fall of the Berlin Wall, that has steadily changed, and the UN now recognises that you cannot have development without having the for-profit sector at the table.

Business did traditionally have some access to the UN and its international work through organisations such as the ILO (International Labour Organization). It is a 'tripartite' body in the old 1950s and 1960s sense of the word – meaning employers, worker representatives and government – which is a consensus building format that addresses issues of responsible behaviour by companies in respect of the employee stakeholder only. The new tripartite system of the modern world comprises of government, for-profit and non-profit sectors.

It was Kofi Annan, as General Secretary of the UN from 1997 to 2006, who brought the for-profit sector into a new dialogue about global development. His father had been a commercial manager for Unilever in Ghana, so Annan grew up in close contact with a multinational that made a positive contribution to his home country. He did not seem to have had the fear of, or hostility towards, international business that so many progressive intellectuals share, and in 2004 he launched the Global Compact to encourage businesses worldwide to adopt sustainable and socially responsible policies.[67] The Compact was in many ways a step on the road to the development of the SDGs and it has welcomed their publication. Today most of the world's development agencies set up by government now say that they want the private sector to be involved in aspects of their work, but they have real difficulty in operationalising that aspiration; in part because they don't have the skills to engage with companies.

The Informal Sector

While this book is focused on relations between the world's three formal sectors, they each have profound and close links with the fourth sector of society, the informal sector. Broadly defined, the informal sector is everything that is not part of the three formal sectors. It is families, friends and local communities doing things for themselves without being part of the formally constituted and legally recognised social system. For many companies, the informal sector is the marketplace of consumers;

for governments it is voters and the mass of ordinary people, the citizens of society on which its legitimacy rests; and for the non-profit sector it is the community generally and the distinct communities of interest around which so many non-profits are formed.

A great deal of the discussion about the informal sector is focused on the economic activity it generates. It is where a vast number of micro-businesses exist, be they a birth attendant in India helping a woman give birth in return for three chickens, or Mexican gardeners in California working for cash. There are a lot of small-scale cash transactions in the informal sector for work that in the private sector would require invoices with taxes added. Consequently governments would like to bring more of the informal sector into the private sector where it could be regulated and taxed. It is estimated that about 79% of non-agricultural employment in Latin America is in the informal sector and, if agricultural work is included, the figure can rise to as high as 90% of the population in parts of sub-Saharan Africa.

In the West, housework is another aspect of the informal sector that feminists in industrialised countries have long argued should be quantified and recognised as a contribution to the economy. Care for the elderly is an interesting example: in developing countries, care for the elderly almost always takes place in the family home and is undertaken by the younger generation. But in industrialised countries much of the care has migrated to the formal sectors. State institutions make provision, while the non-profit and private sectors manage many care homes as an alternative to home-based carers, many of whom operate in the informal sector. The informal sector is the source of many social innovations and business activities that subsequently become formal sector services, and even in industrialised countries it remains a powerful force in society.

It is in the informal sector where hundreds of millions of people around the world make a life and survive, but it is also, particularly in developing countries, where child labour and other major social problems in production flourish. It has been the interface between the informal and formal business sectors, especially in agriculture, where Western multinationals have found themselves caught up in problems such as child and forced labour. On the other hand, the informal sector has a global dimension typical of its poorly measured role in society. Immigrants from developing countries send major cash remittances back to their families at home, for example.

In 2013 the Hudson Institute published a report that showed cash flows to developing countries from the USA, and remittances were valued at $100bn, slightly less than corporate investment at $109bn and much more than the government's contribution in development assistance of $31bn, while private philanthropy contributed around $39bn.[68]

Initiative from the informal sector has its own power to shape society. The Arab Spring in Tunisia was triggered by police abusing an informal sector street trader, and who can forget the sight of Romania's dictator Nicolae Ceausescu being booed from the balcony of his palace in 1989 by the mass of people, only to face death a few days later.

Politicians and governments speak to the people through political campaigns, by passing laws and regulations and introducing taxes to provide for their needs nationally. Many non-profits emerge out of the informal sector because they are close to the people and help to directly meet their needs. Like companies, non-profits advertise their services, seek endorsement and support, while seeking to change public perceptions about the issues that concern them. Furthermore, the informal sector is often the place where many of the great issues of the day will be worked through and decided. Promoting better health through improved nutrition and exercise, or getting the public to save water and do more recycling are good examples of where governments, non-profits and companies have made common cause to change people's attitudes and behaviour for their own and the common good.

For consumer-facing companies, the informal sector is above all the marketplace where consumers live and companies speak to them through a wide range of advertising and public relations techniques. They have their own direct line to the public consciousness and invest a great deal in positioning themselves and their products and services in its mind. Companies can influence the public's attitudes in favour of their products and services but that power can also be used for social and environmental benefit. This ability to communicate directly with the informal sector is potentially a really important aspect of good citizenship, even if it may appear risky for companies to use it to campaign on social issues like recycling, illegal drug use, careful driving or respect for migrants. Some companies have made use of this type of direct communication in association with non-profits and to promote their brand and sales through cause-related marketing, but the power it represents has yet to be fully developed.

When all three formal sectors combine to address issues in conjunction with the informal sector, there is more likelihood of success than if only one of the formal sectors takes up the cause. That is a central proposition of this book. Ideally each country would be able to map issues such as education, health, race relations, recycling, biodiversity, arts and culture and know what each of the other formal sectors is doing and could do. Then there can be a much more coordinated response, with each sector playing the part it is best fitted to undertake.

This chapter has briefly given some pointers to the world the private sector now lives in. It needs to be accepted as part of the process of promoting the common good and in turn it needs to be ready to play its part as a corporate citizen, in contributing to the public good. However, that is not easy to do, as the next chapter explores. There are many practical and some important emotional difficulties to be overcome, before any given society is at ease with its social institutions collaborating for the public good.

CHAPTER 5:

Working Together?

Interaction Already Happens

For business, its early experience of this new global society has been challenging, particularly in respect to relations with the rapidly developing non-profit sector. For example, Shell was pilloried for its stance when the Nigerian government executed a critic of it and the oil industry in the Niger Delta, the poet Ken Saro-Wiwa, in the autumn of 1995. It also had to deal with a very vigorous campaign by Greenpeace against its plan for the dumping of an old oil rig in the North Sea, and despite the fact that it had consulted with government and others about the right approach to decommissioning the rig in an environmentally friendly way, its reputation was trashed on a worldwide basis. Greenpeace was just so much better at getting its story across.

In 1996, BP's operations in Casanare, Colombia, came under attack from non-profits concerned with human rights abuses. In his book *Beyond Business,*[69] the then CEO of BP John Browne says of that time:

> "Watching the media campaign gather momentum was rather like being under siege. BP thought it was a responsible company. We were dismayed to find ourselves accused of complicity in human rights abuses, frustrated that we could not refute the charge of complicity with clear and credible evidence and – because fact and assertions were hard to untangle – fearful that we might never actually find out what truth lay behind the allegations.

> "The situation took up an inordinate amount of senior management's time and energy. Up until this point in my career, I

had not been fully aware of NGOs. Now I could not ignore them. They had become very vocal."

This quote says a lot about BP and Browne's initial lack of understanding of the role of non-profits in society and like a lot of corporate leaders, particularly in the extractive industries at that time, he probably thought that if government had given BP the licence to operate, what the company was doing was just fine. Much to his credit, he changed his outlook as a result of his experience and as a result of these confrontations, corporate awareness of the critical role of non-profits has moved on considerably.

Even so, the interaction between the non-profit sector and business today can still be highly polarised, between outright confrontation at one end of the spectrum, and traditional benevolent philanthropy at the other. BP, for example, has always been a company with a strong commitment to community engagement and giving, and is a major sponsor of the Arts in Britain. However, both BP and Shell have worked hard over the past years at a new model of close engagement with non-profits around economic, social and environmental issues, because both companies recognise their powerful role in shaping society's views.

When I worked as a consultant with Indonesian palm oil producer Golden Agri when it was under attack from Greenpeace, and the Indian aluminium company Vedanta when under attack from Amnesty UK for alleged human rights abuses, I learned just how upset senior executives can be at some of the accusations made about them and their companies. Companies based in the developing world are now experiencing the types of pressures from non-profits that took Shell and BP by surprise. However, this is the price they pay today for living in a more democratic and interconnected world. The answer is not to get mad but to respond to challenges and question the facts, admit problems if they exist, give reasoned arguments in response and take appropriate action where necessary, often in conjunction with non-profits or the government.

These examples of conflict between the sectors on social, economic and environmental issues have come to dominate our awareness of the interaction between them. To the government, non-profits and the wider public, corporate leaders seem especially blind to the negative impact that their business activities are having on the world. In part, that is because they are so tightly focused on the immediate interests of the business and the positive benefits it brings. They don't tend to see the wider context in which they are operating, particularly overseas and they can react very emotionally to challenges.

In addition, the long-term impacts of their decisions are so often not thought through and planned for. For example, single-use plastic has been immensely helpful in getting simple products such as soap, shampoo, clean water and milk to poor people in Asia, but what happens to the waste it creates in societies that don't have effective recycling or garbage disposal systems? It ends up in the oceans where no authority takes responsibility for dealing with it.

In the West, companies expect government to run sewerage and waste collection, that is what they pay taxes for. But in developing countries, governments cannot cope with the problem. Consequently, the companies that trade there have to step forward, as they did in the 19ᵗʰ century in the USA and Europe, to help to build the public infrastructure vital to supporting business success. Companies have to be willing to own their share of resolving the issues and then in partnership with the other sectors, come forward and help create solutions. For example, they could be developing biodegradable packaging and providing consumer education, while governments could improve rubbish collection and non-profits could promote community clean-ups and recycling.

The interaction between the sectors is not all about dealing with the negative impact of corporate activities. The non-profit Gates Foundation for example, has played a powerful role in getting governments and large Western pharmaceutical companies to collaborate in addressing issues such as HIV/AIDS and malaria. These initiatives show that the sectors do interact and bring their own special abilities to the table to create solutions to what previously have been intractable problems. The SDGs can only really be achieved if the corporate sector is a central part of the solution in conjunction with the other sectors, but few are fully ready to play their part.

The interaction between the three formal sectors happens all the time around the world but it is unplanned, ad hoc and specific to a variety of individual circumstances. There is little thought put into country-wide or issue-specific planning for this engagement. The high profile interactions are confrontational, while others are collaborative partnerships and these interactions will continue to happen at all levels of society. They are driven by immediate needs and problems. However, if society is to move beyond this pattern of ad hoc connections, some important inhibiting issues need to be raised and addressed if the combined power of these different types of organisations is to be brought into play in addressing the many problems society faces.

However, there is a real clash of cultures, missions and internal languages between the three formal sectors that needs to be addressed before a more systematic approach to partnership is possible. All three sectors have within them clever people who increasingly share a common education and framework of ideas but often find it difficult to talk to each other in a common language. There are policy issues which divide them and the for-profit sector in particular is often not seen as a legitimate interlocutor because of the profit motive. The hostility towards the for-profit sector in some non-profits in particular is formidable. There are many people in the other two sectors who just don't like 'commercialism' and there are those in the for-profit sector that have very dismissive views of the other two sectors.

Consequently, some of the most difficult barriers to collaboration are much more likely to be attitudinal and emotional rather than purely intellectual. While there are legitimate disagreements about issues large and small between people in each sector, there are other attitudinal and emotional postures that limit engagement. They are rarely recognised and discussed, and in my experience they need to be brought to the surface and dealt with before progress can be made in constructively working together.

It is controversial to apply human psychological thinking, developed in respect of individual people, to large human organisations, but I don't think we can understand these organisations without understanding how the individual human beings within them feel, as well as think. Below is an early effort at surfacing some issues that need much more detailed discussion. They will no doubt be viewed as controversial but the comments are based on years of observing how people within the different sectors seem to respond to each other.

Sector Cultures and Psychologies

Each of the three formal sectors have their own distinctive emotional posture towards the world and each other. In his book *Bad Company*[70], Richard Milton seeks to put:

> "… some of the world's largest and best-known corporations on the analyst's couch, to find out what their unconscious motivations are and how those unconscious emotions have resulted in otherwise inexplicable behaviour – even apparently insane behaviour – in the recent past."

He also says:

> "Companies are like people. Like people, companies can enter into contracts, buy and sell property, make charitable donations, award prizes and even erect memorials to themselves in case we forget about them. Like people, too, companies can be motivated by the entire range of human feelings and human failings: anger, jealousy, greed, incompetence, and fear – fear of failure, fear of disgrace, fear of discovery."

He is right to apply some psychological thinking to the internal life of a company as a distinct corporate entity. However, he should not just apply that notion to companies alone but also to institutions in the other two formal sectors as well. The institutions of each formal sector have their own conscious and unconscious cultures that impact on their internal and external behaviour, and particularly how they view institutions in the other formal sectors and people in the informal sector. From the point of view of this argument, it is more important to analyse the transactions between the formal sectors from a psychological perspective rather than delving deeply into the different character of the diverse institutions of each one.

In this context it is helpful to introduce some psychological insights into how communication and 'transactions' between the sectors might be shaped. In particular, Eric Berne's thinking about Transactional Analysis [71] seems distinctly relevant. While the theory is designed to apply to the interaction between people, I think it has value in understanding important aspects of the interaction between the three formal sectors. The theory incorporates observations about the state of mind (Ego states) of the actors involved in an interaction but then focuses on how they then interact together depending on dominant Ego states at the moment of engagement.

In the book *Games People Play*[72], Berne takes a psychoanalytic view of the human mind and postulates that it has three basic Ego states based on the Freudian and Jungian notions of an ID, an Ego and a Super Ego. It is proposed that they exist simultaneously in any given individual and these states of mind correspond to: the ID as either the 'natural child' the creative and emotionally free child, or the adaptive child who responds to parental influence; the Ego as the rational adult trying to cope with life and negotiating with others to get its needs met and to survive; while the Super Ego is the parent figure, telling the individual how to behave, often based on the beliefs of a distinct moral code.

To some degree these components of an individual human mind are evident as attitudes in the emotional life of the three formal sectors. All individuals and organisations have significant elements of each in their identity but it is the dominant components that influence their posture toward life and other organisations and society in general. Chart 3 opposite sets out this theory in a simple diagram and shows how these Ego states, as Berne calls them, can be applied to the government, the for-profit and the non-profit sector. Each of the parties also addresses the informal sector in its own way but when communicating with each other, the sectors have distinct voices. What we are talking about here is the tendency to a dominant voice and attitude which none of the sectors use exclusively but exemplifies their approach to life.

Following Eric Berne, his collaborator Claude Steiner sets out in his book *Scripts People Live*[73] the idea that people adopt strategies for life which determine their relations with others based on ideas of who they are and how life must be lived. Some of these 'scripts', like that of the alcoholic, are quite tragic in their formulation and lead to serious difficulties in life, not least in relationships with others. He argues that they can be changed but first they need to be identified and understood for what they are.

CHART 3

Transactional Analysis Applied to Sectors of Society

Emotional Postures (Ego States):

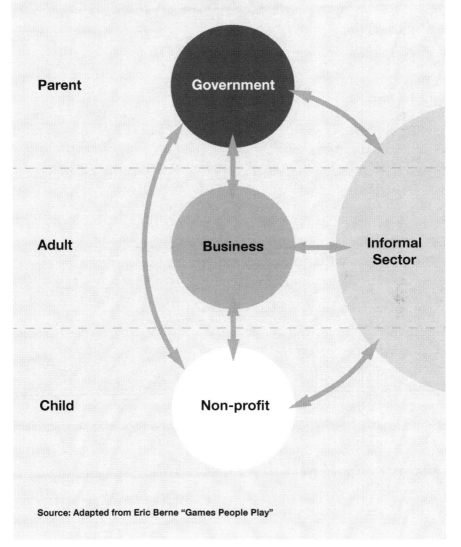

Parent

Government

Adult

Business

Informal
Sector

Child

Non-profit

Source: Adapted from Eric Berne "Games People Play"

There are similarities with how the three formal sectors see their role in society, and in my view they do work to clear scripts based on both an intellectual and emotional assessment of what they think their role in society is. The formal sectors can be resistant to changes that don't fit with their self-image and that can constrain engaging collaboratively with other formal sectors, that don't share their identity. For example, non-profits that serve the community can be suspicious of companies because they serve profit, while companies may see non-profits as do-gooders who live on handouts.

The Emotional Posture of Government

The politicians and civil servants that make up government seem to be strongly inclined to the 'parent' role as their primary posture towards the other sectors and society generally. Governments provide law, order, infrastructure and defence but also tell people what to do. The constant refrain from government to society is one of instruction, backed up by laws, regulations and taxes that say 'send your children to school, drive on the right-hand side of the road, don't smoke cigarettes, exercise, don't over-eat and you can only travel when you have a passport from us.' Laws, exhortation and the control of taxes are key to how government seeks to influence society mirroring how parents behave towards their children in the home.

Governments seem to know what is best for people, what they and other institutions should do for their own good and on occasion are willing to use coercion to get them to do it. As in personal life, there are the 'strict' parents, like many of the world's authoritarian governments. In the West, a good example was Mrs Thatcher. She did not particularly want to be loved, she wanted to be respected. Then there are caring and even indulgent parents in politics too, such as Bill Clinton and Tony Blair. They set out to convince people that they felt their pain and were only doing their best to make life better for them, just as a good parent should. Either way, government makes it clear that it is in charge and makes sure that taxes get paid, laws are kept and good standards of behaviour, as government sees it, are widely promulgated.

This is not to say that the parent role is always bad. People do need the state to intervene on many occasions and there is a legitimate role for governments in creating a framework for communal life and ensuring fair treatment for individuals and institutions. In the former communist countries, a lot of people liked the strict control of life that government exercised; they did as they were told but in turn were looked after in terms of jobs and they had a clear place in society.

The problem for the governmental system is that it instinctively needs to be in charge and set society's agenda, within its own jurisdiction at least. But increasingly it finds it difficult to get people to behave as they should and a number of governments today are experimenting with ideas of how to 'nudge' people and organisations into positive behaviours rather than telling them directly. That is much more difficult to do at a global level, for example, where international companies take advantage of widely varying tax codes to get around local laws. Also, in terms of shaping a dialogue within a country, government needs to see itself as an important party in the conversation about issues not the sole arbiter of the agenda, and that is sometimes hard for elected politicians who feel they have a mandate to lead, whereas in the other two sectors the democratic mandate is not as clearly expressed.

The Emotional Posture of the Non-Profit Sector

In this analysis, the non-profits tend to have one of two postures towards society and the other sectors. First, the service-providing and caring organisations are inclined to be like government but act on a smaller scale as benevolent parent figures. They do everything they can to ease people's suffering, help them along and care for other species and the natural environment. They do everything a caring parent should do and often with real love and commitment. This passionate engagement with people and the environment often leads them to real breakthroughs in how to deal with issues because it taps into the emotions of people, generates new insights and gets them to change their attitudes and behaviour voluntarily. This close engagement gives these non-profits a special status in the eyes of the people because they work so closely with them and are consequently very responsive, also they are not seeking a profit out of the interaction and exist purely to give service; in principle at least.

Non-profit campaigning organisations, on the other hand, have an element of the rebellious child about them. They see injustice in the world and the environment around them being destroyed by the negligent parent figures of governments and companies; consequently they scream out in protest. It was said earlier that many campaigning non-profits will see themselves in the role of the child in the fable who points out that the emperor has no clothes. Ordinary people often admire this stance and when the approval rating of brands is surveyed around the world and non-profits are included, campaigning organisations such as Amnesty International and Greenpeace are ranked much higher in terms of trust than most corporate brands. They are seen to be acting with passion and integrity in the public interest; they are trusted in a way that for-profit companies, politicians and governments are not.

To say that campaigning non-profits have an element of the rebellious child about them is not in any way to disparage them. A healthy ID is vital to the development of a healthy person and campaigning non-profits represent a feeling in society that needs to be expressed. These organisations help to keep the other two sectors healthy by questioning their role in society. They represent an expansion of the democratic process beyond the parliamentary process, just as the campaigners against the slave trade first did, by taking the issues directly to the people. With modern means of communication this role has become truly global. Many in government and companies know they are at a moral disadvantage when dealing with such non-profits because they are 'compromised' by being engaged in the practical business of running everyday life. From a for-profit company perspective, this makes campaigning organisations difficult and dangerous to deal with.

The Emotional Posture of the For-Profit Sector

The ethos of companies in the for-profit private sector is primarily to try and be in 'adult' mode. The sector's basic proposition to society is: "I am selling, are you buying? Can we do a deal?" It is as Eric Berne put it: "I am OK and you're OK"[74] so let's do business! Companies take the view that the market is based on a fair exchange between willing buyers and sellers, with great competition for the buyer's attention, and there is a truth in that proposition. If what a company has to offer is too expensive it will say: "I'll get the price down, if that helps?" or "You can pay over time!" as well as "Have any colour or design you like!" Businesses are deal makers.

The primary aim of the business is to negotiate a deal with an independent third party by listening and responding to what the customer and consumer wants. A deal is to be negotiated between grownups – a willing seller and a willing buyer engaged in a voluntary dialogue with each other. That is why monopolies have been so disparaged since the time of Adam Smith and his critique of the British East India Company. Also, it is not just customers and consumers that are included in this approach but other stakeholders too. Companies have to have the right package of wages and benefits to attract employees and keep them. It also needs to negotiate its relations with suppliers and make attractive offers to investors.

No sector is solely one emotional type or another. They are all a mixture in various degrees and companies use appeals to the public's inner child in their advertising, when they take approaches such as: "Everybody else has one, why not you?" or "This will make you look good!" or buy it "Because you are worth it". They may also use a parental tone in communications, such as: "Use our toothpaste, the dentist says you should!" But whatever twists and turns they use in clever advertising, the deal is still one that has to be negotiated before the transaction can take place and consumers can always say no. Companies cannot make the investor invest or the worker work for them, there have to be incentives on both sides to get the deal done. This is the 'rational', economic self-interest so beloved of economists since the days of Adam Smith, and for companies it very much shapes how they view their role in society.

This emotional disposition has several consequences for the role of business in society. First, it impacts how people are perceived by business as customers in business to business transactions and consumers in the marketplace. With some exceptions, there is a great deal of openness and basic equality in whom companies will choose to do business with. Companies will sell their products and services to pretty much anybody on the planet, irrespective of their nationality, race, colour, creed or gender. For multinationals, this fact gives them a remarkable connection with different sorts of people all around the globe, one which has rarely if ever been exploited for humanity's common good.

For international companies in particular, it is absolutely essential for them to have this culturally neutral view of the world if they want to be successful: the business must embrace the whole of humanity as potential customers, consumers and indeed workers, suppliers and investors if it wants a relationship with them. Consequently, many companies work very hard at extending their offer, often by reducing prices, to include those excluded from the market because they are poor.

Second, companies assume they are dealing with a rational 'adult' customer and consumer, one who knows what is best for them. Fast-moving consumer goods companies, in particular, sell to individual consumers on the reasonable assumption that they are making rational decisions, and that they will use their personal responsibility to manage the consumption of their product or service. The problem is that consumers don't always know their best interests, especially over the longer term. It is others in government, the non-profits that tend to be much more aware of the long-term effects of excessive consumption in matters such as the consumption of salt, sugar, fat and alcohol, for example.

How much money consumers should be 'allowed' to borrow from banks is another such issue that involves both the personal responsibility of the consumer and the social responsibility of the financial services companies. It means companies acknowledging that not all consumers are making rational decisions in matters of debt, their health or how they casually dispose of their plastic waste. There is a real debate to be had about the balance of responsibility between companies and consumers when it comes to many such issues, and the good corporate citizen is the company that acknowledges the issues and gets involved with others, including the consumer, in order to address them.

In this context, private companies that don't acknowledge the issues and resist acting on them can be seen as amoral. They seem to say: "We will give you whatever you want, so long as we can make a profit", a point of view on a par with those selling illegal drugs and sex in the informal sector. There is a whole discussion to be had about the right of individuals to make bad decisions, as well as the role of the state in saving people from themselves, for example, banning the sale of alcohol and drugs. Short of large-scale legislative action and increased regulation, there is a great deal that can be done by companies in partnership with the other sectors and consumers to address problems, and this is where good corporate citizenship is important.

More importantly, there is general agreement about the limits of this corporate view of adult-to-adult transactions, in respect to children. Society will tolerate a much higher level of free market engagement between corporates and adults than they will with children, and rightly so. Children are a special case as their judgment is not fully formed and they are entitled to protection as consumers from offers that can potentially harm them. Here, state intervention is expected in the marketplace, just as it is to ban child labour in the workplace.

The state often takes on the 'parent' role because for-profit companies cannot be relied on to think through and vigorously respond to the abuse of their products and services by children, whether that's in respect of sugary drinks, fatty food, screening out pornography from internet services or addictions to technology. Companies believe in free market transactions between an adult seller and buyer but struggle with the limitations of this attitude when applied to children and young consumers with legally limited personal responsibility.

The other side of this coin is the fact that companies can too readily accept that, when government says it's OK to drill for oil here, or mine, build a dam or power station somewhere else, then they can do it. Authority has spoken, so we are free to get on with what we want to do. This is particularly true in developing countries where companies get their licence to operate from governments but need ordinary people to accept their legitimacy too. Especially if the government is of an authoritarian sort.

Third, this basic posture toward society is in part responsible for the tendency of companies to struggle to think about the medium- to long-term implications of their business activities for society as a whole. Being 'rational' and 'adult' in the conducting of a company's affairs within its own tightly focused but narrow range of activities is a good thing insofar as it makes them efficient and effective institutions. The threat of competition and the need for fine divisions of labour within the workforce are also contributing factors, but if every company only looks after its self-interest, who looks after the interests of the society as a whole?

One of the most defining characteristics of our modern world is the fine division of labour on which it is based. It is a huge strength because it has underpinned so much development and is strongly embodied in private companies, but it is also a great weakness. Companies often see this problem within their own organisation, when marketing doesn't talk to the supply chain, for example, and companies put a lot of effort into getting employees to think outside their 'silo' – and they need to be able to do this in respect to society as whole too. Like government and the non-profits, companies need to see and acknowledge the separate silos in which they operate and seek opportunities for dialogue and collaboration across them. That means organisations in each of the three formal sectors being conscious of their specific strengths, weaknesses and, above all, emotional dispositions and being willing to transcend them.

Companies cannot rely on an inherent free market ideology of voluntary buyer and seller to argue that they have no role in helping to shape the wider development of society over all. Furthermore, if government falls short in its response, or the problem is in multiple jurisdictions and spread across all four sectors, what is the role of the company? If they are passive, then the non-profits will jump in and propose a solution on a single issue basis, which is roughly how the system works today. However, this sort of solution is not good enough, particularly given the scale of company activities, their internal capacities and the tight timeframes the world faces on issues such as climate change. Individual companies and industry sectors need to invest in being much more proactive in considering the longer-term public good and seek to be engaged with government, non-profits and ordinary citizens in the informal sector. However, such collaboration is hard work.

Collaboration is Hard Work

There will always be tensions between the three formal sectors because of their different goals, cultures and emotional dispositions but they are *the* essential ingredients of a truly modern society. The fact remains that each one of the sectors individually contributes significantly to the development of the social whole and, irrespective of their relative size, a civilised society needs all three of them to function well as separate entities and to work together. Consequently, as humanity faces a difficult future, the sectors must overcome their differences and learn to collaborate together in a much more proactive way.

Ideally, each society would develop its own consensus about the relative roles of each sector and seek to ensure that they are to some degree mutually re-enforcing, benefiting from each other's strengths and covering for each other's weaknesses. However, this remains a difficult idea because the debate about the role of the three sectors is highly political. The left still tends to want to expand state control and action, while the right tends to want to promote free enterprise and community self-reliance through voluntary action.

Nevertheless, at the global and national level, humanity needs to find a constructive balance between the work of the formal sectors and, in the meantime, individuals and organisations within the formal sectors need to get on with making relationships work at a practical level. In the case of many developing countries, the best things that international companies can do are to help support the establishment of honest and effective government and to support the growth of an effective non-profit sector.

Collaboration would be better served if more people worked across multiple organised sectors They would consequently be able to understand how each of them work and what they are capable of. Too often people work their whole lives in one sector and do not appreciate what the others have to offer. In the USA, where this model of society has been long established, people seem much more able to move between the sectors, bringing insights and skills from one to another.

People with this sort of experience should be highly prized and hopefully they can play a part in developing a mutual respect for what each sector is good at and be aware of vital differences and limitations. This will help the engagement process while it is still struggling to get established, as will using a facilitator to help broker relations on key issues. The emotional background to the three formal sectors won't change in the short-term and, a bit like psychotherapy for the individual, there are those facilitators who can help the participants in the dialogue get over their instinctive inhibitions about each other.

A good example of the intellectual and emotional adjustment needed to move forward can be found in *Going Green*,[75] a collection of short essays from business leaders and others, about meeting environmental challenges. In it Stephen Tindale, a former Executive Director of Greenpeace UK, talks about his partnership with the energy company Npower. He says:

> "This was an unlikely partnership between Greenpeace and Npower, because on one hand you have a large energy company that still has quite a lot of fossil fuels in its portfolio – it's a burner of coal, which is a very serious contributor to the greenhouse effect. On the other hand, you have a radical campaigning organisation that hasn't traditionally been very friendly with business....

> "...We agreed to differ on the areas of disagreement and cooperate where we did agree – on the common purpose of building a wind farm. I personally take three lessons from this partnership with Npower. First, I was very struck when I met with the then chief executive, Brian Count, that he actually knew a lot more about renewable energy than I did, because he had spent a lot of his career working on marine energy...

> "...The second lesson was that it's been very time-consuming. Working in partnership has often been very frustrating because they see things slightly differently, and there is a lot of working through to iron out the difference...

> "...But the third lesson, the overwhelming lesson is that for all the difficulties, for all the frustration of working in partnership, it has delivered something we couldn't possibly have done on our own. Of course, we could retain our purity and not have anything to do with any of these companies that have fossil fuels in their portfolio, but the result of that would be wind farms would not be built, or they wouldn't be built nearly as quickly."

What is demonstrated here is a much more open and inventive relationship whereby the strengths and skills of each sector are more roundly blended to achieve new solutions to society's problems. The initiative for this cannot just come from government and the non-profits. The private sector needs to contribute leadership too, and in the case cited above, Npower was stepping up to the plate and making a contribution towards finding a solution to the issue.

The earlier quote from John Browne (former CEO of BP) says a lot about how the drive for business success can lead companies to be blind to what is happening around them and, almost by default, they end up abdicating responsibility for their role in helping to positively shape society. Companies are immensely powerful and influential in national and global society but intensely narrowly focused on their business mission and very risk averse in the public arena.

It is time for that to change and in this post-communist period of history, the private sector needs to make a more determined effort to identify and work for the wider common good, first with its immediate stakeholders, but also more widely for society as a whole at home and abroad. It is essential if people are not to continue getting thoroughly disillusioned with private business and repeat the pattern of trying to suppress it. Companies need to have the internal capacity to know where they stand on key issues and how to work with others on the issues that matter to them and the wider society. The next section of this book focuses on how they can do that. Having set a broad context for the role of business in society, it will address the issues involved in managing a business to be a good corporate citizen.

PART 2:

MANAGING THE COMPANY AS A CORPORATE CITIZEN

Introduction

Part 1 of this book has sketched out a view of an emerging global social system based on three organised sectors, each interacting with the others and the informal sector. Most societies have this basic pattern of organisation today and it seems set to go on growing and becoming more established as the global norm. These are the building blocks of the modern world and beneath the ever present turmoil of international politics, trade and economic development issues, they organise and enable everyday life.

The second section of the book looks at how companies can manage their citizenship and play a constructive role in making this emerging pattern of social organisation work to the benefit of themselves, and society as a whole. A healthy business will flourish in a healthy society, and a failure to take a modern approach to the role of business in society may well lead to a public reaction that could see private firms seriously constrained in their activities, or yet again eliminated. Throughout history there has been a repeating pattern of business flourishing and then being suppressed, often because of its own behaviour.

The Reagan/Thatcher revolution of the 1980s was largely about rescuing business from state control, detailed regulation and heavy taxation, then setting it free to do what it did well – produce goods and services for society at a low unit cost. With private companies resurgent, the question has now become what business's role is in society beyond meeting market-driven needs and wants.

The initial answer in the 1980s was to call for an increase in corporate philanthropy and community involvement from these newly empowered private companies. If taxes were to be cut, ran the argument, then companies as beneficiaries should give more to help society. As part of the Economic Recovery Tax Act of 1981, President Reagan, for example, raised the level of corporate profits that companies in the USA could give to charity to 10% of net income, and there was an initial increase in corporate giving and community involvement in those early years of change.[76] However, the corporate commitment to more philanthropy has steadily declined, and today it has slipped back to what is considered the more usual level of around 1% of pre-tax profits; The Campaign to

Encourage Corporate Philanthropy (CECP) and the Conference Board now report it to be at 0.91% of the companies they have surveyed.[77]

Nevertheless, during this early period, organisations such as Business in the Community were set up in Britain to encourage companies to help with unemployment and youth unemployment in particular. Not least because the economic and social changes that were happening were in part caused by large-scale corporate restructuring following Mrs Thatcher's reforms. She, like President Reagan, actively encouraged corporate giving and community involvement and British companies borrowed many lessons from the unbroken tradition of corporate philanthropy and community involvement found in the USA. However, British companies soon realised that the essentially Victorian traditions of philanthropy that flourished in the USA needed to be updated for the modern world. In 1990, six companies formed LBG (London Benchmarking Group), which uses modern quality management thinking and an input/output/impact analysis to do this.

Philanthropy and community contributions were only a partial solution to the great changes that were initiated at that time but they remain a valuable part of good citizenship. As time went by, and in part because of non-profit campaigning, it became obvious to leading companies that it was the total economic, social and environmental impact of the business in society that mattered, not just its voluntary community contributions.

The social and economic issues that affected business were many, such as: plant closures and unemployment as production was sourced from overseas; the need to help young people find jobs; employment conditions in the supply chain and the recycling of packaging. Most significantly, there was growing evidence of the impact of economic activity on the global environment. Large data sets were starting to be accumulated on the use of CFCs in fridges and aerosols and the damage that they were doing to the ozone layer. Urgent action had to be taken to phase out their use and business was key to addressing the issue on a global scale.

In the early 1990s, John Elkington coined the phrase the 'Triple Bottom Line' to encapsulate the economic, social and environmental impacts of business, which became the focus of corporate responsibility and saw the idea of environmental sustainability become established as a goal for companies.[78] The agenda of corporate responsibility and sustainability was exploding as non-profits and the media questioned the impact of company behaviour in the markets, factories and farms of the developing world and beyond. While capitalism had shown itself to be far more inclusive and positive in raising people out of poverty than the marxists ever thought possible, the question now is whether the world can live with the environmental impact of its success.

The short answer seems to be 'no', and how companies are to respond to this challenge is firmly on the agenda. Many responded on an issue-by-issue basis, fighting off challenges when they arose in 'crisis management' mode, but others saw the need for companies to have a set of core values that determine its behaviours beyond the pursuit of a purely commercial mission. The question for debate, particularly for former state-owned businesses, became: what are the values we hold to while doing business? Is a company just about making a profit or is it a 'corporate citizen', sharing with the rest of society its current and long-term concerns? If it is to be a good citizen of society, how does it conceptualise and manage that dimension of its identity?

This section of the book will look at these and other issues, for example, what do we mean by 'corporate citizenship', and why would a company seek to be a good corporate citizen? What is the role of values in defining citizenship and how does a company manage its values? These are all both philosophical and practical questions for companies to address, and I have spent many years wrestling with them.

At its heart, corporate citizenship is about the thoughtful exercise of power in society. Companies have a large degree of power devolved to them to undertake approved business activities, the so-called 'licence to operate' in supplying goods and services to customers and consumers. These activities are at the core of what a company does and virtually every decision it makes. Their pursuit has an ethical or social and environmental responsibility component. Who to hire? Who to fire? What level of wages to pay? What taxes to pay? Where to locate new production facilities and where to source from? What to tell consumers about the product? What images are used in advertising? Are products designed to be recycled or safely disposed of? These are just a few of the decisions related to core business but raise a myriad of wider citizenship questions.

For example, what is a company's responsibility to help wider society with the education of the next generation of workers and consumers? What role should it play in reducing carbon emissions? How does it engage with human rights and gender equality? As a citizen of the societies that sustain it, what role does the company have in sustaining and developing society as a whole? When you set up a business or take on its leadership, you have to be the grownup: you have the power to make the decisions and there is no one else you can blame for them. Leadership involves choices about how to behave, both in business relations and in relations with wider society. This part of the book looks at how to use the power of business as a force for good, because with power comes responsibility.

CHAPTER 6:

What is Corporate Citizenship?

Defining Our Terms

Many other terms are used when discussing the subject of corporate citizenship: corporate responsibility, corporate social responsibility (CSR), Environment, Social and Governance (ESG), or the sustainability and ethics of business. They all have their value and there are fierce debates about which is the right one to use. What they all have in common is a discussion of the role of the company as a corporate entity in society and what responsibilities come with being an important actor within the social whole.

One can take a broad or narrow view of these terms. For example, in the USA, corporate citizenship is often taken to mean the voluntary contributions companies make to society over and above their business activities; their philanthropy and other community contributions are often thought to define good citizenship. In Europe and elsewhere, corporate citizenship is more usually applied to the total impact of business on society and the environment, both within the owned and operated businesses and right along its value chain, from raw materials production to product disposal by consumers. This is the view of corporate citizenship taken here. Companies are 'citizens' of society in a similar way to individuals, they have rights and responsibilities that have to be acknowledged and lived out.

We now talk about 'sustainability' as a key feature of good corporate citizenship and the word has two meanings, of which the first is the most important: environmental sustainability. Since the late 1980s, we have become much more aware of the negative impacts of business and human activities in general on the natural environment, both locally and globally. In 1987, the UN's Brundtland Report developed the concept of environmental sustainability, based on science, which can be assessed in terms of what is taken out of the environment and what is put back, such that a sustainable environmental balance is achieved when resources are not depleted for future generations by their overuse today. It is a helpful and concrete term that gives real guidance to companies about the environmental impact of their business activities.

However, sustainability can also be applied to the longevity and sustainability of the business as an institution, and that is more problematic. Businesses grow, mutate and die in an organic way, and some are not really designed for longevity. Companies have a purpose and when innovation or competition renders that purpose obsolete, they either change or die. Some like Cadbury, were nearly 200 years old, when taken over by Kraft in 2010. That company in turn subsequently split in two in 2011, so Cadbury is not an independent company any more, it is a brand name and part of the portfolio of Mondelez International. This is the 'creative destruction' of capitalism that is a constant challenge to the survival of any independent business, but with all the changes that took place, Cadbury and Mondelez International are still active as corporate citizens in the field of cocoa production because it is a vital part of the business.

Another idea that is important to defining corporate citizenship is the engagement that takes place voluntarily beyond what the company has to do to comply with the law. Voluntary actions and engagement beyond the law are an important aspect of good corporate citizenship but so is keeping the law. Like individual citizens, companies are expected to be both law abiding and willing to make a wider contribution to the wellbeing of society as a whole. It is not either/or, it is both.

Companies and the Law

When a company is incorporated it takes on a legal identity as a distinct institution in society and, like an individual, it is given rights and responsibilities. When framing company law, our forefathers borrowed heavily from the law governing the activities and liabilities of individuals in business and bundled it up with new ideas about limited liability. The idea of the joint stock limited liability company was a social innovation of institutional brilliance. It liberated economic activity and investment from the laws of personal debt and medieval thinking about personal liability.

Joint stock limited liability companies acquired a distinct identity as 'legal persons' jointly owned by their shareholders and an extensive legal framework has been developed around this concept. Company law is still closely tied to the idea that companies, like individuals, have the right to act within the law to pursue their wellbeing and self-interest. For example, individuals and companies should pay their taxes but they also have the right to lobby to have them changed. And, like individuals, companies will make good and bad decisions such as cheating on their taxes.

There are those who are opposed to companies having this legal status as the basis for their role in society. Corporate critic Joel Bakan acknowledges in his book *The Corporation*[79] that companies have a distinct status in society when he says:

> "A key premise is that the corporation is an institution, a unique structure and set of imperatives that direct the actions of people within it. It is also a legal institution, one whose existence and capacity to operate depend upon law. The corporation's legally defined mandate is to pursue, relentlessly and without exception, its own self-interest, regardless of the often harmful consequences it might cause to others. As a result, I argue, the corporation is a pathological institution, a dangerous possessor of the great power it wields over people and societies."

Bakan sees corporations as amoral institutions only concerned for themselves and their shareholders' profits. He argues that they are therefore incapable of concern for others and, in that sense, they are psychopathic and must necessarily be so. Kent Greenfield makes a more nuanced but similar academic argument in his book *The Failure of Corporate Law*:[80]

> "For much of the history of the United States, 'public' corporations were deemed to have important civic responsibilities. At the beginning of the twenty-first century, however, 'public corporation' is amongst the most misleading terms in all of law or

business. In my view, the public should have a much greater say in how corporations are governed. Notwithstanding the terminology, public corporations are typically seen as private institutions, and the law governing them is considered a branch of private law (along with contract and property law), which governs relationships between individuals."

It is a key premise of this book that companies have choices about how they behave and this section of the book is about how they develop the capacity to make good choices. Even if the two writers quoted above got radical changes to corporate law to make companies somehow more accountable to society, there would still be a debate about what constitutes good corporate citizenship in everyday life. In addition, the law is never all-embracing, it can be interpreted very differently by different lawyers and, in so many of the situations that companies face, it is not an absolute guide to action. The law so often trails far behind the best practice of good corporate citizens.

In addition, while companies should in general keep the law, what do they do when faced with situations such as apartheid in South Africa? Or women's employment rights in Saudi Arabia? Or China's lack of law on independent trade unions? Furthermore, the law is often used to set minimum standards on issues such as wages, reporting, insider trading, environmental and advertising standards and much more. While minimum legal standards are important because they are applicable to all companies, they are often slow to be formulated, and leading companies often voluntarily go well beyond them. International standards are increasingly important and may well need to be consulted in cases such as child and forced labour in many developing countries, but they are far from comprehensive on the environment, and the UN and other international bodies have a limited capacity to enforce them.

The analogy between individual companies and an individual citizen has its limits but it is useful when thinking about the role of companies in society. We want ordinary people to have the freedom to live their lives as fully as they wish but they need to do so within a framework of law, and then beyond that to be responsible for the consequences of their decisions both for themselves and others. We can pass laws about the use of seatbelts in cars, but the main thing is to get people to believe that using them is the right thing to do so that they use them willingly and the state is not expending massive resources to enforce the law.

While law has a crucial role in shaping society, there are limits to what it can do about other aspects of personal behaviour such as what to eat, how often to exercise and how much alcohol to drink. Governments and others know that encouraging personal responsibility in the decision-making of individual citizens is a vital challenge. Similarly, we need individual companies to be thoughtful and effective in managing all the consequences of their business decisions. The movement within business to create 'B' corporations with an overt commitment to society, workers, the community and the environment, in addition to making a profit, is a sign of this trend today. Even if it is a small movement right now, it has spread around the world and in English-speaking countries in particular.[81]

Corporate citizenship is a term that recognises the company has rights and responsibilities but puts it on notice that, just like individual citizens, companies need to acknowledge wider responsibilities to society rather than just acting from pure self-interest. If we just look after ourselves, who looks after the whole? And contrary to what many in business think, that is not just government's job. It is the job of each individual and, indeed, each organisation in society. The preamble of the Universal Declaration of Human Rights, for example, recognises this and calls for governments, all other organisations including businesses, and private individuals to play their part in ensuring it is adhered to. To be a good citizen, corporate or individual, is not just about keeping the law, it is about being an active participant in shaping and sustaining society as a whole.

It is not just companies that are 'corporate' citizens within society, all organised bodies incorporated in law are 'corporate' citizens too. Just like companies, incorporated bodies are a body of ordinary citizens (a 'company' of people) organised around a specific purpose to benefit themselves and by implication, society generally. Incorporated bodies of all sorts, like businesses, are part of that wider society that sustains, and in turn that wider society also needs to be sustained.

A university is a corporate citizen of the local community and a citizen of the wider world of academia it inhabits, as is a hospital, a school, a church and a charity. Even government offices and institutions such as prisons have a distinct corporate identity, one which necessarily has a symbiotic relationship with the society and the environment around it. This relationship needs to be acknowledged, mapped and understood as an obligation to be taken up as an extension of the organisation's primary purpose. Even if its purpose is one of public service, a university, for example, it can contribute so much to a local community through its job creation, supply chain and voluntary activities to help educate local people and the wider community.

Stakeholders and Corporate Citizenship

In Chapter 3 it is argued that the widespread acceptance of stakeholder theory by companies today has contributed to them developing a wider view of their role in society. At the heart of the debate about good corporate citizenship is the question of how companies treat their stakeholders. While investors own the business, and in law have the rights of ownership, other groups such as consumers, employees, suppliers and communities have a big 'stake' in the business.

Consumers rely on the safety and quality of products and can suffer from price rises; employees depend on the business for wages and could lose their jobs; suppliers can lose contracts or not have their bills paid on time; and communities can be devastated when a plant closes. They all have a stake in the fate of the business, just as the shareholders can lose the value of their investment or suffer from poor dividend returns on their shares. Like shareholders, stakeholders have a tangible economic interest in the company that can be mapped and measured. Consequently, a responsible and well-managed company thinks long and hard about the impact of its decisions on these groups of people because they are so closely connected to the company and its success.

Similarly, with the environment, it has become increasingly usual to add the physical environment to the list of such stakeholders. It too is very much affected by business policies and decisions, and environmental sustainability has become part of company stakeholder thinking and mapping. While it often falls to scientists and environmental activists to speak up for the physical environment and other species, they are articulating a plea for consideration that companies need to listen to, just as it should to any other stakeholder. Interestingly, the ethics and values that we use when thinking about the interests of human stakeholders are increasingly being applied to the physical environment and other species. The environment is seen as having an intrinsic worth, just as human beings do, and the moral precepts we apply to human relations are now widely accepted as applying to forests, rivers, mountains, whales, pandas and the millions of animals in the human food chain.

The above list is widely recognised as a company's core stakeholders but it is not exhaustive and each company will have its own list, depending on its identity. A pharmaceutical company, for example, will have close links with universities and the worldwide community of research scientists and doctors, who also have a 'stake' in the company and its behaviour. They are concerned about where it spends its research money, how it conducts its patient trails and its transparency about scientific data. Stakeholders are not immune to wider systemic pressure within the global free market system but companies can often act to mediate their impact on their stakeholders, for example, by phasing in price rises due to currency devaluations. Well-managed relations with stakeholders is a primary test of good corporate citizenship.

Acknowledging that corporate responsibilities go beyond those owed to shareholders as owners, and embraces a wider group of stakeholders, has been an important step forward in business philosophy. Stakeholder theory has broadened the vision of the role of business in society significantly. It has strengthened the idea that corporations are citizens of society with wider responsibilities, not just profit-making engines for their shareholders – many of which only hold shares for a matter of weeks or days. Stakeholder theory has given companies a broad base of connection with society and forms the basis of an approach that can be expanded further.

Empowering Stakeholders

Corporate citizenship has two distinct elements: first, the role companies have in society as distinct corporate bodies, but second, the role they can also play in promoting and supporting the citizenship activities of their different stakeholders as well. When a big company passes on its knowledge and shares its resources with stakeholders, it is empowering them and using the relationship it has with them to expand its own sense of citizenship. This relationship can be immensely powerful in society, given a company's reach to consumers and its connections with suppliers along its value chain.

At a simple level, this could be enabling employees to volunteer in the community on company time or matching the cash gifts they give to charity as Levi's did with its Community Involvement Teams in its sewing plants. I have also seen this outreach to stakeholders in various forms in many companies, for example, Unilever Ghana seeking to reduce fatalities at work by training drivers in defensive driving, joined with its transport suppliers and shared costs to put supplier drivers through the same training that was provided for Unilever drivers.

Further examples of empowering stakeholders also include Unilever helping small retailers selling the company's ice cream to replace their CFC-based fridges with new non-polluting ones. While the international alcoholic drinks company Diageo supported bartender training to help low-income people get jobs, give good service and help manage consumers at risk of abusing alcohol. Diageo also helped the customs authorities in developing countries to fight corruption and better manage the import of drinks and other products. NatWest's small business advisors in Manchester helped ethnic minority business customers plan for the transition of their business to the next generation within the family, while The Body Shop and Apple help their customers recycle their packaging and even core products.

In the past, multinationals and other companies in the developing world would take on the problems of a society and solve them for their employee stakeholders. They created huge corporate welfare states with housing, healthcare, education, shops, transport to work and even law and order in the community for those employees on which the business depended. In return, the employees became totally dependent on the company. ICI Explosives based in Gomia, Bihar in India, was a classic example of a company town developed to support the business, but when the company needed to downsize its operations due to disruptive forces in the marketplace, I worked for it in an advisory capacity on winding down the immense commitment to employees and others in the community. In some ways weaning the community off dependence on the company was a lot harder than winding down the business itself.

However, this old model is dying out, partly because of cost, but also because it is deeply paternalistic. Companies today need to have strategies to help employees in developing countries build their own houses, buy bicycles to ride to work and shop at independent small stores. The employees need to own their own assets and not be tied to the company that is providing them. This also applies to the local communities that need schools and clinics for everyone, not just company employees. As was the case in Gomia, setting up non-profits to provide these services instead of the company, was an important solution to the community impact of the downsizing. For less than the cost of providing everything for workers and others, companies can have a huge influence on local societies by reaching out and empowering their employees, communities and supplier businesses.

The Wider Society

Engaging with stakeholders can directly benefit the company in many ways and be motivated by corporate self-interest, and this is often the case. Mutual benefit is a powerful incentive to action. Private citizens who do things for family, friends and neighbours in the informal sector, may well enjoy a reciprocal benefit at some time. However, they can also reach out to others about whom they know little, and have no contact with, and companies can do the same. The public support for disaster and famine relief in far-flung parts of the world is a prime example. People will respond when they see suffering and they want to help. Good corporate citizens are the same – they can respond to need when they see it around the world, even when they have no direct relationship with those who are suffering.

Some corporate outreach to the wider global society is genuinely altruistic, for example, the disaster relief programme organised by Diageo. This highly organised system was developed to respond to major disasters around the world and has been active in communities and countries as far-flung as flooded New Orleans, where its speedy intervention was praised by the US Congress, the Sichuan and Haiti earthquakes, cyclone Larry in Australia, and even the Ebola outbreak in Sierra Leone.

Diageo is not a brand name and its premium brands probably have very few customers among the people of Sierra Leone. As a drinks company, Diageo knows a lot about water and its Water of Life programme has taken clean drinking water to more than 10 million people in countries such as Burkina Faso and Ethiopia, again not big markets for its products. It has practised genuine outreach based on the perception of human need and the core competence of the company, whether working closely with international and local non-profits or just on its own.[82]

In recent years, there has been a tendency for non-profits concerned about the great issues of the day, to dismiss corporate philanthropy. They tend to say: "We want to talk about the impact of your business not your good works". It is fine to want to understand the total impact of business activity along the whole value chain but a small but significant aspect of good citizenship is the philanthropic outreach that companies do. It is not an either/or situation, it is both. And the 10 million people who now have clean water courtesy of the Diageo Foundation would probably agree. Corporate citizenship has many aspects to it and the broad societal issues that are not tied directly to the business, such as disaster relief, the plight of refugees and the education of girls in developing countries, speaks to our common humanity.

Mapping the Scope of Corporate Citizenship Today

Philanthropic outreach aside, the scope of corporate responsibility today is defined as the total impact of the business on society and the environment. Companies have begun to accept the 'triple bottom line' of economic, social and environmental impacts of the business as being their special responsibility, and these three factors stretch right along the complete value chain of the company from small farms in Indonesia to small shops and consumers in New York. 'From field to fork' is a phrase often used in the food industry and that includes incomes for small farmers at one end of the value chain and the recycling of packaging at the other – which, if you are a Coca-Cola or Starbucks, are very big issues. Chart 4 opposite shows how economic, social and environmental issues are spread along the complete value chain of a notional consumer-facing food company.

The company itself is placed in the centre of the value chain and it manages its backward linkages through the supply chain to a myriad of suppliers around the world. Issues range from the prices paid to farmers for crops, the use of child labour, and the impact of pesticides on food quality and the environment.

Chapter 6

Once the company has acquired the raw materials it needs, it then needs to source manufactured goods such as packaging to support its products after it has manufactured them in the owned and operated business. It then sends products out on the various paths to retailers and the ultimate consumer. Here, in the forward linkages of the value chain, there are questions about retailers' margins and the prices charged to consumers. Also, social questions such as, does the food foster childhood obesity or diabetes? And environmental questions like how to handle the disposal of packaging. Some of these are determined by law but many by the willingness of the company to engage with them and develop solutions, often in partnership with others.

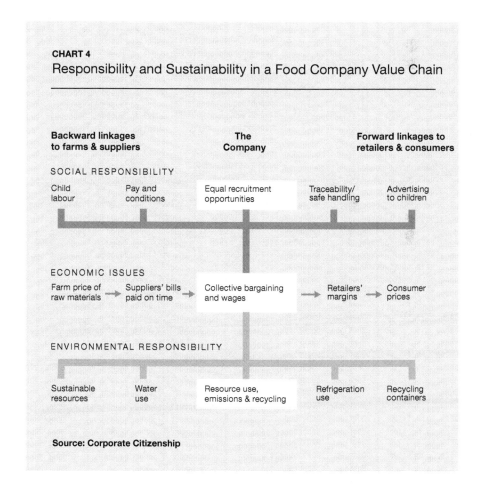

CHART 4

Responsibility and Sustainability in a Food Company Value Chain

Backward linkages to farms & suppliers		The Company	Forward linkages to retailers & consumers	
SOCIAL RESPONSIBILITY				
Child labour	Pay and conditions	Equal recruitment opportunities	Traceability/ safe handling	Advertising to children
ECONOMIC ISSUES				
Farm price of raw materials	Suppliers' bills paid on time	Collective bargaining and wages	Retailers' margins	Consumer prices
ENVIRONMENTAL RESPONSIBILITY				
Sustainable resources	Water use	Resource use, emissions & recycling	Refrigeration use	Recycling containers

Source: Corporate Citizenship

In the past, the primary definition of good corporate citizenship was focused on the owned and operated business at the centre of the chart. That is the company itself, and the activities that it had full control over, how it treated direct employees was of particular importance. In that case accountability was clear. However, once lengthy supply and distribution chains developed around the world, the problem of accountability and control became much more complex.

Cadbury had a fine reputation for the social responsibility of its business in the UK and particularly how it looked after its workers, but how does it monitor the social and environmental conditions affecting the one million cocoa farmers in Ghana who produce the large majority of its cocoa? In colonial times, Cadbury virtually ran the cocoa business in Ghana according to its business principles, but today it now has only a few employees based there and it cannot act alone to identify and address issues in cocoa production. Cadbury and Mondelez, the parent company, must work with others in government and the non-profits to protect the brand and see that its values are lived out at the extreme backward end of its value chain.

The non-profit community and international NGOs have done much to pressure companies into thinking about their responsibilities all along the value chain and in global supply chains in particular. Like the anti-slavery campaigners before them, they have helped redefine what is responsible corporate behaviour by pointing out the complicity of global companies and brands in economic, social and environmental abuses around the world. They have issued a wake-up call to businesses to see themselves as good citizens, to be active in mapping their responsibilities to their stakeholders and the wider society and doing something about the issues that impact on them. The scope of corporate citizenship now has a global geography as well as a triple bottom line dimension.

Companies are Human Institutions

The idea of corporate citizenship also has a wider implication for companies precisely because they are not just economic entities designed to make a profit for shareholders. Whatever economic theory and the laws of ownership say, the reality of life within a company is a much more varied and human one. It is true that in order to stay trading in the free market, companies must make a profit but they are much more than just amoral, money-grubbing machines. They are important social organisations in themselves. They are made up of ordinary citizens with their own moral codes and standards. People live their lives through companies and they care about what a company may do in their name. Today, we have a much more educated, informed and connected world population who sees companies as important social institutions that can act for the common good if they choose to.

In a post-communist world, it has been all too tempting for the leadership of business to think that all people want are the goods and services they so efficiently provide. Companies have been successful by being tightly focused on their business mission and all this talk of economic, social and environmental concerns seems like a distraction to many business leaders. Also, companies are under great competitive pressure in global markets and are afraid that they are being dragged into areas of life in society where they feel they are not competent to judge and lack the capacity to act.

The notion that the business of business is purely business was never a very viable one and, in our modern world, it is not at all useful. Modern media and campaigning non-profits make it impossible to keep the corporate head down while waiting for things to change. Companies need to accept that stakeholders and society want them to be proactive as corporate citizens, helping society to face immense problems worldwide. They want them to do this as well as continuing to provide vital goods and services to meet people's needs and wants. Good business and good citizenship are not an either/or, they are both and should be mutually supporting.

The leadership of modern companies needs to accept that society wants and needs them to be a force for good and to then put some real intellectual ability and financial muscle behind that commitment. First and foremost, this means owning a share in the many issues that touch on the business and its stakeholders and organising resources to deal with them, often in partnership with others; then reaching out to contribute to meeting society's many challenges. Companies employ some of the world's cleverest and most competent people and many of them will welcome the challenge of using their company as a base for contributing to the development of wider society, and what they do, may in fact help it to be more successful. The following chapters are about why and how a company can play its role in society as a good corporate citizen.

CHAPTER 7:

Why Be a Good Citizen?

Openness About Motives Is Vital

Not one of the three formal sectors has a monopoly on solving the world's problems, but together they each contribute something different and valuable when formulating solutions. The future is about building a distinctive way of problem-solving using the institutions of the three formal sectors. Pining for a utopian solution is going to continue, but in the reality of everyday life the pragmatic approach is to encourage active participation in the dialogue of all three formal sectors. However, getting the for-profit sector and the global multinationals, in particular, ready for this role is a challenge. They have immense material and intellectual resources but they are tightly focused on their commercial self-interest and are often not really available for engaging in collaborative activities, even if the other two sectors want to invite them in.

However, it does not mean that all three sectors must always work together. Often two sectors, such as the government and business, will work together on an issue such as worker retraining, while business and non-profits will work on community job renewal. It is pretty rare and difficult to organise all three sectors to join forces to address a problem, but it does happen. For example, the employment of marginalised groups such as ex-offenders or the seriously disabled requires government funding for non-profits to engage private companies in creating employment opportunities. What is important is that each sector knows what the others are doing and the role they should be playing on key issues. This is where trust and mutual respect between the sectors is a key feature of the approach.

While some companies do make a wider, positive contribution to society, many are much more reluctant to take up such a role. They see it as a distraction from the relentless focus on the business success and the bottom line. Competition is a key feature of the for-profit sector and there is a fear that if only a few companies devote resources to being engaged, the others will stay more focused on the bottom line. Business people can easily see time and effort spent on corporate responsibility and sustainability work at a cost. They rarely calculate the benefits it can bring in a world of highly educated, globally connected consumers, employees, opinion formers and regulators. Why should companies do the right thing? This is endlessly asked within business and doubts about corporate motives in the other formal sectors are a major barrier to corporate engagement with others in society. It is important to be transparent about this issue in order to build trust and move forward.

So many people question company motives and think that doing the right thing and being engaged with society is just about public relations and above all, reputation. Having a good reputation is a very important motivator for companies in a competitive marketplace; it is vital to commercial success. As Facebook found out in 2018 when the crisis over the apparent misuse of its users' data, wiped $60bn off its stock price and caused an 18% drop in its revenues. Company reputations can be fragile and failures in responsible behaviour toward stakeholders can have significant effects in both the short and long term. Having a good reputation is an important motivator for companies to act as good corporate citizens, but it is not the only one.

There are a variety of motives for companies to be good citizens, and they vary widely and are sometimes a compound of more than one. It is important for companies to be clear with themselves about their motives for good corporate citizenship and to communicate them clearly to the other formal sectors and the wider public. People will accept self-interest as a motive for activity and engagement, but only if the companies are honest and open about it. Set out below are some of the reasons why companies might want to do the right thing and be good citizens. It is not exhaustive but it is designed to give the reader an insight into why companies would want to do the right thing.

Different Motives for 'Doing the Right Thing'

There are several reasons why companies would do the 'right thing' in their relations with stakeholders and society. Motives can vary widely between being based on highly ethical imperatives or on pragmatic cost saving or market building initiatives. These latter motives are often called 'the business case' for responsible behaviour, which is important, but companies cannot limit the discussion to topics of concern where the numbers add up for the business. Doing the numbers is always important for all business decisions, even citizenship ones, but to only act on issues where the numbers add up raises major issues in itself. Sometimes companies do the right thing just because it is the right thing to do, irrespective of cost or lost opportunities. The different motives for good corporate citizenship and ethical behaviour in companies are often mixed rather than being pure, and I don't think that matters.

The key reasons below are ones that stand out as shaping a company's character as a corporate citizen and motivate it to act well in society. They are as follows:

• **The Founder's Values**

Many of the companies that attract attention for being 'good' do so because the founder established an ethical culture in the company that was real and has outlived them. For example, at the front of her book *Body and Soul*[83] about The Body Shop, Anita Roddick says:

> "I am still looking for the modern-day equivalent of those Quakers who ran successful businesses, made money because they offered honest products and treated their people decently, worked hard, spent honestly, saved honestly, gave honest value for money, put back more than they took out and told no lies. This business creed, sadly, seems long forgotten".

Like the Cadbury and other Quaker business people before her, Anita Roddick built a business and a global brand based on her and her husband Gordon's sense of social and environmental responsibility. So too did the ice cream company Ben & Jerry's. They had a mission statement with three parts that first committed to quality product, second to financial sustainability and then third said: "Our social mission compels us to use our company in innovative ways to make the world a better place". In practice, this meant care for supplier farmers and local communities where the company gave minorities jobs and franchise opportunities. Their competition included Haagen-Dazs, which competed with some of the sexiest ice cream adverts ever seen in the media, and it also did well. Consequently, it would be misleading to say that good values are the only way to build a business.

However, business founders and leaders do have choices about their priorities and social and environmental responsibility can have a real economic value in terms of the trust it builds with employees and consumers especially. Some business founders also get great satisfaction from doing the right thing; using the power they have in running a business to be a force for good. They feel their lives have been a bit more worthwhile than simply chasing the bottom line.

Once established by a founder, the ethos of social responsibility can live on long after they have left the business, as is the case with companies as diverse as IBM, Johnson & Johnson, The Body Shop, Tata and Unilever. Managers, graduates and workers are often attracted to such companies precisely because their founder's values are still alive and informing how the business is run. A key factor in keeping them alive is to make them explicit, when the founder moves on or dies. Robert Wood Johnson did in 1943 when he wrote the J&J Credo, which is set out below in The Importance of Values section of this chapter.

In my view, companies whose founders are truly committed to doing the right thing for stakeholders have a predisposition to success but it is still not absolutely certain. Commercial reality is hard, and competitors may make better commercial decisions. All too often those companies that do the right thing for the right reasons don't talk about it much; modesty is a virtue after all. Few people today know about Levi's stance on racial equality in the workplace in the USA of the 1950s, or Cadbury's cash premium for cocoa growers in Ghana in the early 1900s, long before Fairtrade was thought of.[84] When founders act from a sense of values they do so 'for the right reasons', not because it is good public relations, but that should not stop them publicly sharing their experience and talking about what they do. They can act as role models for other companies.

• Building the Business

Lord Lever, one of the founders of Unilever, was a classic Victorian entrepreneur with a strong sense of values who strove to do the right thing by his stakeholders. In his book *The King of Sunlight* [85], Adam Macqueen describes how Lever displayed a profound sense of responsibility to employees and strove to enforce good standards of treatment for workers in the supply chain for palm oil and coconut oil. His example influenced the ethos of the company through to the modern day. However, modern managers need much more accurate and up-to-date information to show that social and environmental responsibility can help to build the business and there is plenty of it among modern stakeholders.

In 2017, Unilever published a study based on 20,000 consumers around the world that showed 33% of them were choosing 'responsible' brands and 20% actively seek out such brands. Of Unilever's hundreds of brands, ones such as Dove, Hellman's and Ben & Jerry's, which have integrated sustainability and social responsibility into their purpose and products, grew about 30% faster than other parts of the business. The study also suggested that while 53% of consumers in the UK felt better for purchasing a sustainable product, the figure was 85% in Turkey and Brazil and 88% in India. Sustainable and socially responsible brands were driving 50% of the company's global growth.[86] In its report *The Values Revolution*, Global Tolerance claims that 50% of people prefer to buy from an ethical company and 31% say they are willing to pay more to do so.[87]

The worldwide awareness of the need for corporate responsibility and environmental sustainability is growing across all stakeholders and companies can tap into it to grow their business. In terms of employees, the Global Tolerance report says that 42% of all individuals and 62% of millennials want to work for a company that makes a positive impact. With regard to shareholders, in 2016 the *Global Sustainable Investment Review*[88] said that there are now $22.89tr of assets being managed as part of various forms of responsible investment strategies around the world. This is 26% of all managed assets worldwide and Japan was the fastest growing market.

Using corporate responsibility to grow a business is much more fully discussed by Professor David Grayson in his book with Adrian Hodges, *Corporate Social Opportunity!: Seven Steps to Make Corporate Social Responsibility Work for Your Business*.[89] From this brief review of the evidence, it is clear that there are opportunities for companies to make social and environmental responsibility pay dividends for the business.

• Saving Costs

More hard-nosed business people may have little sympathy with high-minded ideals of social responsibility but they do respond to initiatives that save the company money. Levi's is a company that has a long-established sense of values derived from its founding families. In the early 1980s the city was in the grip of an epidemic known as Gay Related Immune Deficiency Syndrome or 'GRIDS' – later it was given its proper name HIV/AIDS. The leadership of Levi's treated the grim situation facing gay men working for the company as a human rights issue requiring compassion, understanding and immediate action, irrespective of costs. Levi's engaged in partnerships with other businesses, health professionals, gay activists and the mayor's office to address the problem and senior managers took a strong public stand on the need for action, long before the Federal government had really stirred.

Many years later, a public health activist colleague Alice Lamptey and I addressed the Ghana Employer's Association on the subject of HIV/AIDS, and her highly articulate appeal for compassion, social solidarity and the national interest was met with hostility and indifference by many. Some actually stood up and said that the virus was God's punishment on sinners. Many in the room saw the emergence of HIV/AIDS as a social issue and nothing to do with business.

I spoke next as a European and an outsider – knowing my limitations in that social context, I expressed no moral opinions at all. I simply showed 15 slides projecting what would happen to business costs if HIV/AIDS spread in Ghana as it had in East Africa, where infection rates were more than 20% of the adult population. All the companies in the room paid healthcare costs and the cost of an AIDS patient to a business over time was huge – it could wreck profitability. More companies volunteered than we needed to help us with workplace pilot programmes and, in this case, it was cost saving that was the great motivator for action, not moral conviction.

This is true in so many areas of corporate life, be it saving energy by changing the light bulbs, reducing water consumption, reducing packaging and waste to landfill (now taxed), companies save money and help the planet too. Helping a developing country to improve water and sanitation in poor areas can help reduce worker absenteeism due to water-borne disease and thereby increase business productivity. It pays to keep workers healthy and if the company is not going to provide its own water supply for its workers, engaging with the community is the other way to do it.

The interests of a company and society can align on a wide range of social and environmental issues, so that doing the 'right thing' saves the business costs, avoids disruption and contributes to productivity. There may be expenses involved in such initiatives, but the financial benefits produced for the company can more than offset the initial costs and money is saved in the short to medium term.

• Promoting Mutual Benefits

In the past, large companies in particular have been prepared to pick up a range of costs that have mutual benefits to the business and society, particularly in the communities where their operations are located. Employers no longer build their own towns as Lord Lever, the Cadburys and Milton Hershey in the USA did. However, Paisley in Scotland was gifted much of its civic architecture by the Coates family who made thread there; Cummins Engines virtually built Columbus, Indiana; and Jesse Boot led the building of Nottingham University. Why did they do this? It seems it was a mixture of civic pride allied to investment in the long-term development of the community where the business was located.

As Boots grew, it was in need of skilled chemists, lawyers, accountants and managers and the costs of the university were thought to be worth the 'return', however long-term and indirect that was. The investment in the university made the town more attractive to managers and, while none of the graduates from the university were obliged to work for the company, there was a local pool of qualified labour to call on.

This engagement with society is often seen as philanthropy but it is much more like 'community investment', as the LBG styles it: an investment that benefits the community but also benefits the business in the longer term. While the world was admiring Andrew Carnegie's philanthropy (a model of disinterested 'giving back' that came to dominate US thinking about corporate social responsibility), Peter Drucker points out that Sears, Roebuck and Co. was 'investing' in the education of American farmers and their wives across the USA, enabling them to be more productive farmers and thereby earn more, so that they could become better customers.[90] An updated version of this sort of approach has been articulated by Michael Porter and Mark Kramer in their work on 'Shared Value'[91] activities by companies, where working with society can enhance business performance.

Cause-related marketing is also a modern way to promote a social benefit by involving consumers in causes such as HIV/AIDS, as The Body Shop did when it combined with MTV to reach millions of under 25-year-olds in 44 countries.[92] Not only does it raise money for a good cause but it also educates people about the issues. Taking corporate responsibility and citizenship into the marketplace is an important development. In the past, it has tended to be focused on other stakeholders, particularly employees and communities, but consumer power is of growing importance and cause-related marketing is only one way of engaging consumers in the issues.

• Unavoidable Challenges

Generally speaking, companies are risk averse when it comes to tackling important social, economic and environmental issues. However, everyday life will confront companies with ethical, social and environmental challenges whether they like it or not, and it is best to be prepared. Hand-wringing denials don't work when the broad mass of people feel the company has responsibilities in a social or environmental situation. Companies are part of society and as it develops they are invariably caught up in its struggles to define and act on issues, particularly ones which companies themselves have helped to create, such as the filling of the oceans with plastic rubbish or inequality in employment.

Ed Cray's book *Levi's*[93] gives a good account of how the company faced down racism in America in the 1950s. At that time, Levi's was expanding rapidly and building factories in the Southern States of America, where racism was endemic and enshrined in law. Walter Haas and his brother Peter, who together led the company, saw that they had to confront the issue because it was against their values to perpetuate discrimination in their plants. Quietly and cautiously they succeeded in creating equality of employment in their plants and dealt head-on with one of the most pernicious problems of American national life. Plants were established in poor rural areas in the South that gave industrial jobs to local people, paid them decent wages and helped them send their kids to college. Not only did the company help local people economically, it helped them to learn to live together.

The leadership of Levi's had seen the reality of the racial discrimination in society and, as employers, they could not avoid owning a share of it. They could not avoid the ethical issue and they did what they could within their sphere of influence to address it. No great financial costs were involved, although there were social risks locally and in the marketplace, but the company did the right thing in identifying and addressing the issue. As corporate citizens, companies are part of society and, like it or not, have to deal with all the issues and dilemmas that society faces. So, it is best to be prepared and know why and how to respond.

• It is Just the Right Thing to Do

There is a certain amount of overclaiming about what corporate responsibility can do for a business. If a company behaves well it is said there will automatically be benefits to the business and its reputation, but at what cost? Sometimes the costs are extremely high, and then it takes real courage to press on and do the right thing, but in many cases it pays off.

The classic case is that of the extortion attempted against J&J over the cyanide poisoning of some Tylenol capsules in 1982, and as a result seven people died in the Chicago area.[94] The company response was to recall every Tylenol tablet from all of its stockists in the USA and destroy them. This was a huge cost to J&J estimated at $100m at the time, but it was the right thing to do, and within a year the brand had bounced back in the marketplace. In addition, the reputation of the company as an ethical business, concerned first and foremost with the wellbeing of its customers, was decisively enhanced.

More recently, Ray Anderson describes in his book *Confessions of a Radical Industrialist*[95] how, in response to the world's growing ecological crisis, he bet the whole future of the carpet tile business he founded on moving from oil-based carpet tile production to an ecologically sustainable one. He says:

> "It all started with Paul Hawken's book, 'The Ecology of Commerce'. I read it, and in the course of a single night all thoughts of retirement, of travel, of chasing a little white ball vanished. The institution of business and industry was thoughtlessly destroying this world, yet business and industry was the only institution that could lead a movement to save it. If business and industry had to lead, who would lead business and industry? Unless somebody did nobody would. Why not us?"

He was responding to one of today's big issues and committing a huge amount of management time and resources to address it, and from 1994 to 2007 the company struggled with the challenge. It found that cost savings could be made from environmental adaptions but that was not what motivated the change or the huge financial risk involved. It was the values of the founder and the company he came to believe in.

In Asia, Indonesia's largest palm oil company Golden Agri was the subject of an intense campaign by Greenpeace that focused on the problems associated with the rapid growth of the palm oil industry. Deforestation, the opening up of high density peat lands (which is bad for climate change), the loss of biodiversity and particularly the decline of the orangutan were all of concern to Greenpeace. It really got Golden Agri's attention by persuading its business customers, including

Unilever, Mars and Nestlé, to stop doing business with it. Golden Agri responded in several ways, including setting aside a considerable amount of its landholdings for conservation purposes.[96]

This action came at a real but publicly unquantified cost to the business, but the company's desire to be world-class in its business practices was a key driver for change and it was prepared to absorb the costs. Other factors were an awareness of a changing attitude in Asia and around the world to the value of the environment, especially among the young; the reputation of the business and the family that owned it; and indeed the reputation of the industry and how that reflected on the reputation of Indonesia as a country.

Companies do the right thing, then, for various reasons. Some are purely pragmatic – it can help grow markets or cut costs. Or at the other end of the spectrum, it is because of core values that companies will incur significant costs and take major risks to do what is right. Often it is a mix of the two. However, there is no question that the real key to doing the right thing in society is for a company to have a core of values that enable it to identify and act on vital issues. Furthermore, on important occasions, to put social responsibility above profitability in a way that the East India company never could.

The Importance of Values

Values lie at the heart of the discussion about corporate responsibility and sustainability. They guide the exercise of power and are the foundation stone on which it is based. Every individual citizen, whether they acknowledge it or not, can only live in society because they share certain values and beliefs with others, and the same is true for corporate citizens. Any group of human beings that comes together to undertake a task, project or lifelong commitment, will find that in order to work together there has to be some sort of consensus on basic values. Without those basic values, a group will fall into conflict and disunity. Values are so often a prior condition for collaboration and collective action of the kind that drives companies in their everyday work. Whether they acknowledge their values explicitly or not, companies have them. They are fundamental to their corporate culture.

In the USA, with its written constitution, there is a predisposition for leading companies to be explicit about their values. Thomas Watson Jnr wrote an entire book about values called *A Business and its Beliefs*,[97] based on his experiences at IBM. More recently Tom Chappell, the founder of Tom's of Maine, wrote *The Soul of a Business: Managing for Profit and the Common Good*.[98] In his book *Confessions of a Radical Industrialist*[99], Ray Anderson speaks eloquently about the role of values in helping him to transform his business. The *Mission Statement Book*[100] by Jeffrey Abrahams reproduces 301 such statements from American companies and they are well worth reviewing; however, many companies conflate their commercial mission statements with ethical and values statements in a way that many non-Americans might find difficult to accept.

To be tightly focused on the commercial purpose of your business is vital to business success, but so is detailed knowledge of the values the company lives by while pursuing its commercial goals. A business must make a profit to survive, but at what price? Even Milton Friedman, who denied that companies as institutions have social responsibilities, said that while the primary mission of a company is to make a profit for its shareholders, it must do so in an ethical way. A values statement defines what 'ethical' is and can be as broad or as narrow as the company wants to make it.[101] Economic activity and ethical considerations are inextricably linked but they are not identical and it is important to acknowledge that almost every business decision has an ethical, moral and citizenship aspect to it.

In businesses founded by entrepreneurs with strong values, such as Anita Roddick or the Cadbury family, it is the founders and owners who decide the values of a company. Just as at Levi's, where the owning families made it clear that they want to do well and make a profit, but not at any price. They will not exploit child and migrant labour and will do everything possible to avoid damaging the environment. The founder/owners can infuse the business with their values but the problem with concentrating the definition of these at the top of the business is that a charismatic CEO cannot be everywhere in a global economy. As a business grows over time, and the founders withdraw from management, so it is vital to write down and codify company values. In this way every employee and other stakeholder can see what the business stands for and therefore hold it accountable to its own stated values, as well as law and social norms.

One of the finest, simplest and most direct statements of values is the J&J Credo, and it is quoted in full below. It was written in 1943 by Robert Wood Johnson just before the company went public. It was his and his family's way of codifying their approach to doing business. As such it was a guide to the growing group of professional managers that increasingly ran the business around the world. It clearly and simply sets out the values that underpin the relationship between the company and each of its stakeholders in turn. Stockholders for example can expect a 'sound profit' not a maximum one and suppliers and distributors must have the opportunity to make a 'fair profit'. The Credo creates a complete framework of values that shows managers how the company should behave when confronted with choices that have an ethical dimension to them.

However, just as society is always evolving – after all, slavery was once considered a normal state of affairs, as was the exclusion of women from the political process and much of working life – so too the Credo has slowly developed. In 1943, when it was first written, women were primarily responsible for childcare and its first sentence instanced a responsibility to mothers but was subsequently expanded to include fathers as a recognition of their changing role in childcare. Changes will be made to any value statements but slowly, because basic human values are in many ways slowly evolving.

Box 2

The Johnson & Johnson Credo

"We believe our first responsibility is to the doctors, nurses and patients, to mothers and fathers and all others who use our products and services. In meeting their needs everything we do must be of high quality. We must constantly strive to reduce our costs in order to maintain reasonable prices. Customers' orders must be serviced promptly and accurately. Our suppliers and distributors must have an opportunity to make a fair profit.

"We are responsible to our employees, the men and women who work with us throughout the world. Everyone must be considered as an individual. We must respect their dignity and recognise their merit. They must have a sense of security in their jobs. Compensation must be fair and adequate, and working conditions clean, orderly and safe. We must be mindful of ways to help our employees fulfil their family responsibilities. Employees must feel free to make suggestions and complaints. There must be equal opportunity for employment, development and advancement for those qualified. We must provide competent management, and their actions must be just and ethical.

"We are responsible to the communities in which we live and work and to the world community as well. We must be good citizens – support good works and charities and bear our fair share of taxes. We must encourage civic improvements and better health and education. We must maintain in good order the property we are privileged to use, protecting the environment and natural resources.

"Our final responsibility is to our stockholders. Business must make a sound profit. We must experiment with new ideas. Research must be carried on, innovative programs developed and mistakes paid for. New equipment must be purchased, new facilities provided and new products launched. Reserves must be created to provide for adverse times. When we operate according to these principles, the stockholders should realize a fair return."

The word Credo is a religious term and embodies the 'creed' or beliefs that the company lives by. The Credo clearly came out of the personal conviction and vision of Robert Wood Johnson and the owning family. However, among other things, by articulating these values, the Credo helps to prepare the business for a role as a publicly owned company with a global presence. Values such as these are equally vital to large secular, public companies such as Shell. It has a lengthy code of principles plus an even longer document giving guidance on how to interpret that code. This guidance is vital to managers in the diverse cultures of our global economy who may join a firm and know nothing of its history but a well-written code gives assurance to employees and others as to the spirit in which to conduct business and maintain relations with the wider society.

The initial Cadbury Code of Business Principles was written by a family member but as the business grew and time moved on, it too needed updating and I worked on that process. While a core document in itself, the code also forms the basis for subsidiary documents and policies such as Cadbury's Ethical Trading and Human Rights policy.[102] This policy took one or two sentences from the main code of business principles and expanded them much more fully to address human rights and ethical trading practices in the company's immensely complex global supply chain. This was a specialised code which, once written, was field-tested around the world in countries as diverse as Mexico, China, Indonesia and Ghana to see if it could be applied in such a variety of cultures. This is of some importance in a global context, not least because people around the world need to be clear as to whose values it is that we are talking about.

The Cadbury policy avoids the accusation of 'Western liberal imperialism' in part because it has been tested against the situations of diverse societies around the world, but most importantly because it was carefully benchmarked against the UN Universal Declaration of Human Rights and relevant supporting international conventions. These have been adopted by a great many countries and therefore are applicable in their jurisdiction whatever cultural norms might be. By signing the various conventions different countries have aligned themselves with a set of universal values, the very ones companies should be observing.

When addressing the politically sensitive issue of human rights with suppliers in China, for example, we were able to point out that its policy reflected the UN conventions on human rights that China itself had signed up to. Consequently, Cadbury was asking the Chinese supplier to share evidence that they kept to international standards on labour matters, just as it kept to international standards in food production, food quality and water treatment. However, China does not endorse certain UN conventions relating to independent trade unions, so in this case Cadbury company values came to the fore. It was argued that workers in China, as elsewhere around the world, need channels of communication with management over and above those provided by government-recognised official unions, and the supplier was asked what measures it took to give workers such a voice.

The Values Cascade

Once a company is clear about its mission and values, they have to be turned into practical reality. Most ethical statements have more than a hint of aspiration to them and for these aspirations to become real, detailed policies or supporting codes of practice, such as a supplier code or marketing code, are essential. It is then possible to measure the performance of the company against its own values and report openly on how it is doing. Chart 5 opposite shows how values cascade down through the business to a level where aspirations become measurable and performance can be communicated.

The arrow alongside the cascade points both ways because the majority of the flow of ideas about responsible behaviour is down from the values statement or code of principles to detailed policies and practical operations on the ground. However, even corporate values change by exposure to real-life experience, as in the case of the J&J Credo. So as the world changes, so must companies, and from time to time they need to re-articulate their values based on practical experience in the world around them. Companies live in the 'real world' and need to be sensitive to its changing sensibilities. This is an area where engagement with non-profits and campaigning NGOs can have a real effect on corporate thinking. Non-profits can truly be 'the canary in the coal mine', warning of changes to come and allowing companies to begin to adapt their values and policies.

CHART 5
The Values Cascade

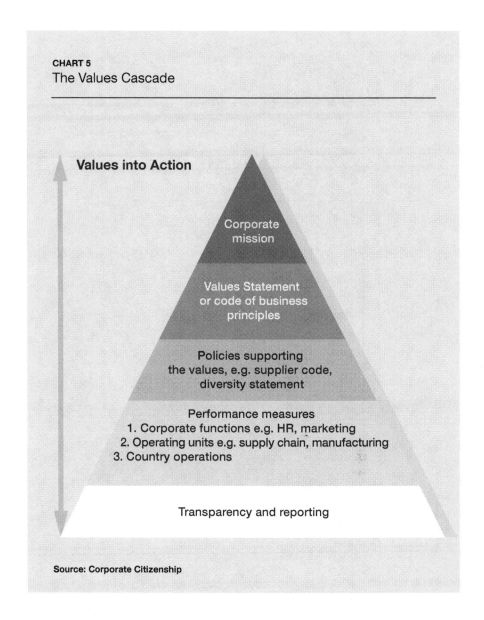

Values into Action

Corporate
mission

Values Statement
or code of business
principles

Policies supporting
the values, e.g. supplier code,
diversity statement

Performance measures
1. Corporate functions e.g. HR, marketing
2. Operating units e.g. supply chain, manufacturing
3. Country operations

Transparency and reporting

Source: Corporate Citizenship

The most important thing about having clear values stated complementary to the business mission, is that it makes the company's ethical and citizenship issues susceptible to a modern management approach. It takes important issues out of the realm of philosophy and opinion, creating a concrete framework of facts by which to judge a company's performance as a responsible corporate citizen. Chart 6 below, shows how this can be done.

CHART 6

Managing Values: Measure and Benchmark Performance

The health and safety of employees as an example

Values and Principles	Key Issues	Measures	Benchmarks
" We are committed to safe and healthy working conditions for all employees "	▲ Safety monitoring systems in place ▲ Health monitoring systems in place ▲ Employee training undertaken ▲ Who is an employee? What about contractors?	▲ Number of training days ▲ Lost time/accident rate ▲ Sickness/absence rates ▲ % of sites audited ▲ % ill health and retirement ▲ Fatalities at work	▲ National average by type of employment ▲ Industry average by type of employment ▲ Best in industry ▲ Awards gained ▲ Inspectors' reports ▲ Prosecutions

Opinion Data: Surveys of employee views on health and safety performance

Source: Corporate Citizenship

Working from left to right, we can set up a value statement, identify the issues it raises, measure performance based on key performance indicators, benchmark that performance in various ways to give it a context to the company's relative position on the issue, and finally then take into account appropriate opinion data from stakeholders. This process will indicate how the company is living out its values and how much improvement is needed, if any.

Most of the information in Chart 6 is hard statistical data within the competence of the company to generate. In respect of worker health and safety, the 'Lost time/accident rate' is important and companies will have that themselves. Also, they can often find such data from other companies in order to get an industry average and a 'best in class' company performance on the issue. However, benchmarks can often be societal norms or industry averages, and this data may well depend on governments and others to generate it and consequently may not be available, particularly in developing countries.

Consequently, the final box of Chart 6 for opinion data becomes particularly important to the relevant stakeholder. For example, if an oil company in Africa says it is committed to providing a safe and healthy workplace, there will be few published local benchmarks to judge it against and therefore asking the employee's view makes sense. If 90% agree with the statement then it is probably true, but if that figure is only 50% then there could be a serious problem that is worth investigating.

In our work with companies, we constantly find that they do not collect data on wider social and environmental issues, so when challenged they find it hard to respond. With regard to the use of child labour, for example, challenges came thick and fast in the early 2000s and Unilever did not collect data on the age of the youngest employees worldwide, so it was hard to respond to allegations that it existed in countries like India.

However, once this was done, it was clear that there was no underage employment in Unilever companies worldwide. In fact, it was countries such as the UK that employ 16-year-olds, while in developing countries like India, the age of entry to employment in Unilever was 18. While not a problem on the ground, the company's Code of Business Principles was subsequently amended to make it absolutely clear that child and forced labour were not to be tolerated within the business or its supply chain. Which immediately expanded the scope of the data Unilever, Cadbury and other such companies needed to collect from suppliers.

Companies don't like surprises and to find that data is requested by non-profits on issues like forced labour, modern slavery, the gender pay gap, water use and deforestation requires them to collect the data but above all think about the issues and their connection with them. If the data is not readily available, companies become concerned for reputational and other reasons and will start to collect it. The old adage is true, 'if it is not being measured it isn't being managed'. Companies then have to integrate the data into an overview of their performance, see what is learned and think about the issues in relation to the company's overall mission and values.

The Need for Openness About Performance

If companies are to step up and form partnerships with government and non-profits, they need to educate their potential partners and the wider public about their values and how they operate. They need to be much more transparent about how they run their business, what they think about their responsibilities in society, and what they do about them.

The annual financial report is primarily a report to one stakeholder, the shareholder, and it won't fulfil that job. Fortunately, the growth of corporate responsibility and sustainability reporting has begun to address this issue. Sustainability reports can sit alongside financial reports and show how companies live their values around the world. At their best, they are a chance for companies to share rarely seen data on responsibility and sustainability issues and discuss more openly with stakeholders and others, the dilemmas they face in running the business responsibly.

Sustainability reporting is relatively new and still developing. The initial demand for it came from activist non-profits wanting to shape corporate behaviour by promoting disclosure about the company's economic, social and environmental impacts. Consequently, the type of data and style of presentation rather limits the accessibility of these reports as far as consumers and the wider public are concerned. That is a distinct communications challenge for companies. While non-profits and campaigning organisations are a legitimate audience, companies need to be able to communicate their values and citizenship more widely.

The expansion of the Global Reporting Initiative (GRI)[103] based in the Netherlands is a good example of how this trend is growing worldwide and the willingness of companies to support it. Within the GRI system, corporates and non-profits have collaborated to set standards for sustainability reporting by companies on a worldwide basis. This is a good thing in principle but because of its campaigning non-profit origins, GRI tends to be focused on 'bad' company behaviour.

For example, the questions it asks on behalf of consumers tend to be about corporate failures, such as product recalls and legal infringements in advertising codes, rather than asking how many more people managed to get vital products such as hand-washing soap and mobile phones this year compared to last. Nevertheless, developing a global standard for reporting and measuring corporate responsibility and sustainability is a positive thing, but companies need to be able to articulate their all-round contribution to society, and particularly to consumers.

Another major problem of the emerging global trend to sustainability reporting is that it is largely driven by a need to respond to 'global stakeholders', which in reality means international campaigning groups and others. Socially Responsible Investors (SRIs) in particular need this sort of data, in addition to financial data, to be able to show why one company is more responsible than another and therefore can be included in their portfolio. These international stakeholders want and need aggregate global data on performance, and sustainability reports provide this.

However, national governments and most importantly, people around the world want to know what the company is up to in their country, and there is a real need for multinational companies to share information on their activities in specific countries, but only a few companies have made the effort. Unilever, Diageo, SABMiller and Coca-Cola all have done some good work here but there is much more to do if there is to be a really effective dialogue across the sectors on a country by country basis.

This gulf in knowledge and understanding between the organised sectors urgently needs to be bridged, and one of the best examples I have worked on was the project jointly undertaken between Oxfam and Unilever, to assess the total economic and social impact of the Unilever business in Indonesia. Having signed a confidentiality agreement, Oxfam was given open access to the workings of the Indonesian company and all its business data. Oxfam had started its enquiry with a view that the company was sending home profits to rich investors in the Netherlands and that was not good for Indonesia. Meanwhile, Unilever was proud of the jobs it created, the investment it made in the country, the taxes it paid and the wide range of affordable goods it provided for the local people. The dialogue lasted two years and it was not easy, but both parties learned from the experience and the report detailing the work was published.[104]

The highly educated and motivated Oxfam staff learned, for example, that the company did not pay a dividend every year and that, over a five-year period, dividends were about 38% of gross profits; the rest of the gross profits stayed in the country as taxes and reinvestment, and 7% of dividends went to local people. With respect to jobs, about 2,500 jobs in Unilever-owned factories supported about 100,000 full-time equivalent jobs back down the supply chain to small farmers producing a range of raw materials; while approximately 200,000 jobs were created in forward linkages from Unilever factories in the paths to market, mainly through small family-owned stalls and shops. The company consequently had a big impact on local society and, even so, the report does not take into account the health benefits to the Indonesian people of Lifebuoy soap, for example.

A particular strength of Oxfam in this project – and it is something that companies have to learn – is that they and other non-profits are good at asking second order questions about the jobs that Unilever was proud of creating. For example: were they good jobs with decent pay? How much influence did Unilever have on the employment practices of others in its value chain? This questioning alerted Unilever to a number of issues that it needed to address in its supply chain and that was a positive outcome from the engagement.

The report produced remains one of the best examples of close collaboration between a multinational and a non-profit. It drove home the importance of quality engagement across the sectors to address economic and social questions. Even so, more could have been done as the report did not tackle environmental questions, and neither was government involved in the process. The government had a separate agenda with Unilever which was concerned with small business development and job creation, and that was working well. With the publication of the report, parties external to the company in Indonesia and beyond had a true overview of its impact on society and so did Unilever itself. The report gave the company, for the first time, a clear overview of its impact on one country and an indication therefore on what that wider impact might be globally. A follow-up report on the South African business added to our knowledge of how the company impacts local societies.

CHAPTER 8:

The Management Challenge

Developing the Capacity to Contribute

Companies not only need a clear sense of values and acceptance of their wider role in the world, they also need the internal capacity to be able to understand the issues and act on them. Their engagement in society cannot just be led by a few senior executives responding in an ad hoc way to non-profit pressure. Companies need to develop the internal capacity for a sustained proactive stance towards society. Private firms will go on providing the goods and services society needs and wants but they know to add the ability to act as good corporate citizens in a regular and systematic way.

Although business is set up to 'serve profit', I hope enough has been said to show that business also serves society through their commercial activities and beyond. However, if companies are to think beyond their immediate commercial self-interest, we need to develop a new management discipline of social responsibility and sustainability management. Just as in the post-war years, partly under pressure from leftish thinking and trade unions, companies had to develop a modern approach to human resources based on management science. Today, companies must develop the internal capacity to identify and manage their economic, social and environmental impacts directly and in partnership with others. It is the price they need to pay for their ongoing 'licence to operate' and living their values. In addition, there is of course, the potential to reduce costs and also to grow the business.

Companies as Agents of the Market

It is tempting to discuss the world's problems in gross aggregate terms – climate change, mass extinctions, economic inequality, mass migration, patterns of trade and investment, the workings of the property market and food shortages, for example – and more is said about these types of issues in the next chapter. But many of these problems arise out of the everyday decisions of ordinary people and also through the everyday decisions of individual companies. They are the agents of the market, and they shape it and are shaped by it.

The previous chapter has shown how companies can take much more control of their role in society and shape their business decisions to contribute constructively to the common good as well, and fulfil their primary business mission. They need the values and management science to know the significance of their decisions. What is proposed here is not the answers to society's problems, but good corporate citizenship has the capacity to be an important contributor towards finding those solutions.

Large international companies are some of the most powerful and important institutions on the planet, touching the lives of millions of stakeholders in multiple countries. Similarly, a multitude of small family companies are a powerful presence in small communities. Each of them has a distinct 'agency' and can make choices about how to fulfil their role in society. They will be vigorously pursuing their business mission but with a sense of values and the internal capacity to act on them; they play a role in society and contribute towards its general development and success. While they will most often do that by addressing the issues close to the commercial identity of the business, they can also transcend them and contribute more broadly to the general good.

Managing Citizenship

Companies have responded to globalisation with immense energy and speed for commercial reasons. They have reorganised their supply chains and mobilised international labour markets in a quite extraordinary way. They have also expanded to open up vast new markets and this process is continuing today. They have followed their business mission into the global economy and created the in-house capacity to do it.

However, they have only moved haltingly forward, often under non-profit and government pressure on understanding and managing economic, social and environmental issues that their activities are linked with. At moments of crisis, they have made progress on reinterpreting their relationship with society in facing up to major environmental issues such as CFCs and the ozone layer. They have also made progress on social issues such as equality in the workplace, but the issues keep coming: real wages are static in developed countries, innovation is destroying jobs, plastic waste is swamping the oceans and electronic waste is mounting up everywhere as people worldwide consume a vast array of new means of communication.

When companies have responded to such problems it is often in an ad hoc way and focused on single issues as a result of a crisis. However, now is the time for them to become much more systematic about managing a broad range of relevant and important issues. A company can only claim to be a good corporate citizen when it has the values and management systems in place to show it fully understands its role in society and is actively managing all aspects of its relationship with society and the environment.

Today we need a new branch of management science to show how this is done. In writing about the emergence of how management science generally became an established discipline, Peter Drucker notes that the first-ever management science conference was called by Herbert Hoover and the President of Czechoslovakia in Prague in 1923.[105] He says:

> "Yet it was not until my 'Concept of the Corporation' (1946) and 'Practice of Management' (1954) were published that management became a discipline accessible to managers all over the world. Until then each student or practitioner of 'management' focused on a separate area: Urwick on organisation, others on the management of people, and so on. My books codified it, organised it, systematized it. Within a few years management became a worldwide force."

We are in a similar position today with respect to the emergence of social responsibility and sustainability as management disciplines within the company. Their development will follow that of logistics, quality control and human resources, which were barely recognised as distinct management disciplines in their time but they are now properly established and play a vital role in businesses. Companies do move forward and clarify how aspects of corporate responsibility and sustainability are managed as they arise, but it is rare for a company to articulate a clear, positive stance as a corporate citizen and demonstrate the management systems that sustain it.

It is beyond the scope of this book but we need a new Peter Drucker to thoroughly systematise the management of this emerging area of corporate life. Whatever companies do in future, we will build on what has been developing in the past 40 years or so as companies have been feeling their way forward towards a new relationship with society. Now is the time to take a more proactive stance in managing that relationship at home and abroad, throughout the value chain of the business. Several key developments stand out as being foundation stones of progress and they are discussed below.

Leadership From the Top

It is a cliché, but true to say, that leadership from the top of a company on these issues is vital. When I joined Levi's in 1980, it had a Corporate Responsibility and Ethics Committee made up of the senior officers of the business (Chairman, CEO, Chief Financial Officer and Chief Operating Officer and a Board non-executive family member). It was essentially a management committee rather than a board committee but it existed to review and address a wide range of ethical, social responsibility and environmental issues necessarily raised by all sorts of business decisions. The Haas and Goldman families who led the business (it was both a private company and a public one during my time there), had strong values. They wanted to run a successful business but not at any price. They knew that many business decisions had ethical and social responsibility elements to them so took care to have a system in place to identify, review and act on them, in parallel with everyday business decisions.

This sense of 'corporate responsibility' was not only a product of the leadership values but also part of the general social contract between business and society in the USA. Business was free to get on and do what it did, so long as they behaved responsibly, 'gave back' to society and engaged with its great issues. This was in fact part of the vision of President Reagan and Prime Minister Thatcher but it largely got lost in the rush to take advantage of the new opportunities that they helped open up. To have companies play a larger role in society roles requires them to make some investment in internal management systems necessary for them to do so in an informed and useful way.

Those management systems need to start at the top of the company and increasingly public companies are creating board committees to have oversight of social responsibility and sustainability within the company. This is a positive and growing trend in the West because such a committee gives status to the issues and it creates high-level accountability for performance. These committees are often chaired by a non-executive director who is well-placed to provide strategic guidance for the business and CEO about citizenship strategy and longer-term priorities. Most importantly, if substantial costs are involved in certain decisions, then it is a board committee that can recommend them.

Such committees are also a signal to investors and socially responsible investors in particular that the company takes these issues seriously and is seeking to manage them in a coherent way, even if there are costs involved. In an article for the Ethical Corporation in February 2013 Professor David Grayson and Andrew Kakabadse share research on how the FTSE 100 Companies managed social responsibility and sustainability at the top of the business. They found that 34% of the companies had a board committee for corporate responsibility, 17% had a committee led by a board member and 18% said that the board had oversight of the subject.[106]

After the board, the role of the CEO is crucial because they have a broad overview of the company's place in society and are best placed to articulate its values. Indeed, there are those who say the first responsibility of a CEO is to manage the company's values. A CEO such as Paul Polman of Unilever, has a high profile in these matters. He draws on a history of corporate responsibility at the company and articulates the connection between the long-term future of the business and the future of global society and the environment. CEOs are vital to this debate and give it real importance, especially when they are supported by their boards.

Within the business and without, people listen to what top business people say about key issues because they are highly educated and their comments are based on their direct experience at home and abroad. Furthermore, it takes a visionary CEO such as Ray Anderson of Interface to lead from the top and develop a new strategy to move the company away from petroleum-based products as a primary input to an environmentally sustainable base and turn it into a viable sales offer.

CEOs can set the tone and articulate the company's values and champion key issues but their main responsibility is to create a system within the company to manage these issues. CEOs cannot and should not do everything, especially in global companies. They cannot see or know the company's relationship with society, multiple different cultures and the environment around the world and, by holding too much power in these matters, can in fact hamper the ability of others in the company to act. However, CEOs do have the special ability to make sure all types of activity are drawn together and articulated in a coherent way for the business as a whole because they may see further from the top of the corporate pyramid.

In his book *Connect: How Companies Succeed by Engaging Radically with Society*[111], John Browne the former CEO of BP makes this point forcefully when he says:

> "Rethinking organisational design goes to the heart of this book's main recommendation: it is only possible to integrate society's needs by changing the roles and responsibilities of teams and individuals. The most important point here is that societal and environmental issues must be taken on by core commercial functions. This starts with the redefinition of the CEO's role but it must cascade down through the company so that people 'in the line' consider the wider context as part of their day-to-day activity. That is the only way to ensure that vital external forces are addressed by high-performing, powerful executives rather than people in CSR who may not 'get' business."

It is true that the line managers and ordinary employees of the company are engaged with the realities of ethical and sustainability problems on a daily basis. However, like all employees, they are busy people and not necessarily financially incentivised to focus on challenging wider citizenship issues. Furthermore, those issues can be very complex and managers are not necessarily prepared to deal with them. Those responsible for making important corporate decisions range from board committees and the CEO, to frontline and country managers who may, for example, be moving sourcing to China for cost reasons but won't necessarily know about the human rights and environmental issues that such a decision raises. They need someone to turn to for detailed advice and that person is not the CEO, who is busy and doesn't necessarily know much about the issue either. It is here that good CSR departments that focus on the ethical, economic, social and environmental impacts of the business can help the company manage the interface with society.

An Internal Management Capacity

Criticism of CSR departments, see below, is generally ill-founded. Critics talk grandly about wanting social responsibility integrated into the business, not kept in a small separate department. But it is not an either/or situation, it is both. It is true that companies need their line managers and employees to be aware of their values and concern for sustainability and social responsibility, but often the questions raised are not just 'moral' but highly technical in character and need careful analysis based on research and a detailed understanding. Managers and employees are trained to be highly focused on a particular business discipline and do not necessarily have the awareness, skills and external contacts to address the wider citizenship problems they face. And that also depends on whether they have been able to recognise them as problems in the first place. Managers and employees need to be able to find help and support from within the business just as boards and senior managers do.

The increase in the number of corporate responsibility and sustainability departments in the past 20 years has been a good step towards improving the quality and range of corporate engagement with society. These departments can be a focus of specialist knowledge and contacts that can help the company identify and address issues. They can act as internal consultants to their management colleagues, fully immersed in the culture of the company but charged with understanding its position in society and helping formulate the company's response as a good citizen. It is not easy to make the case for the expansion of corporate staff at a time when companies have been cutting them back, but a few anthropologists, economists, political scientists and non-profit staffers on the payroll could well be worth the cost, for international companies in particular.

Even John Browne, who is strongly opposed to the existence of CSR departments, recognises this dilemma when he says:

> "However, while CSR units should be abolished altogether, companies will still need staff to analyse stakeholders and examine trends in society's expectations and behaviour. That work should serve as an input into the decisions of commercial managers, who have their own, more senior, engagement responsibilities. There is also a balance to be struck between head office control and local freedom. The former can ensure a coherent approach to outsiders, but executives on the ground have a much better understanding of the local context, of what realistically can be achieved."

Having worked in and advised CSR departments, three distinct roles stand out for them. First, acting as a researcher and advisor to the board committees and senior leadership of the company. Senior management know how to run a successful company but often need help to analyse and make ethical decisions in respect of the many economic, social and environmental matters that business has to confront. Detailed staff work is often required on citizenship matters, just as it is on financial and human resource matters, because it is often vital to aid both good business and ethical decision-making.

In my time with Levi Strauss & Co., disinvestment from South Africa under apartheid was a good example as there were significant business costs and loss of opportunities to be weighed up. Similarly, with the decision to close plants and impact local communities. The key role of the tiny CSR department was to do just what accountants and lawyers do – namely the 'due diligence' on key business decisions with citizenship components. The CSR unit did the ethical, economic, social and environmental analysis on key issues alongside other managers who looked at financial and other business aspects of the problem.

Second, these departments are an internal resource for line managers facing difficult day-to-day business decisions that don't require big policy initiatives. One of my first jobs in San Francisco in 1984 was to help the head of corporate factoring deal with a major credit default by a bankrupt retailer in the central valley of California. The manager had done his job well and got a lien on the property of the retailer, so all Levi's debts were covered, but the owner had absconded with a great deal of cash he was holding for migrant workers. If the company took all the value of the property, which it was legally entitled to do, the migrant workers would get nothing.

Together we ran the numbers and put a proposal to senior management that we should allow the courts to share the value of the property with the migrant workers and it was accepted. The company took a loss but did the right thing in ethical terms. In turn, the factoring department was able to keep its record of good credit control in respect of defaults and no performance bonuses were adversely affected.

I had a similar experience with the head of children's wear who needed to get a labour-intensive product into the market at a specific price point and could only do it by outsourcing production. That would almost immediately lead to the closure of a children's wear plant she had worked with for years. She knew the workers well and really felt the pressure of the decision. It was a heart-rending situation but we were able to work the issues through with senior management support. The plant did eventually close because the labour component of children's wear is much higher than basic jeans but the market pressure was mediated to make change more manageable over time.

In both of these cases, the ordinary managers had a sense that the company would want to do the right thing in a tight situation and needed specialist help to figure out what could be done, given the realities of a market economy. Neither of the managers knew the details of the company's social responsibility policies but both knew the company had a strong sense of values and that the internal consultants in the CSR department were there to help them work through the problem. The decisions we came to enabled the individuals concerned to live with their conscience, and the company as a corporate citizen to behave with integrity while still pursuing the commercial business mission.

Third, CSR departments can act as horizon scanners for emerging economic, social and environmental issues that may soon be important for the company. One way they can do this is by building close relations with non-profit groups that are working on, and campaigning about, social and environmental issues. As a newcomer to the San Francisco head office of Levi's, I was given one of those tedious jobs that no one else wanted to do – responding to questioning letters from small non-profits and major religious bodies asking questions about how the company behaved towards various stakeholders, particularly employees and suppliers.

By engaging with religious groups and non-profits, I was in effect engaged in horizon scanning for issues and emerging concerns in society, such that we were helping the business to prepare for a changing economic, social and environmental context. This is a key role for any business because so many are caught flat-footed by issues that even the most cursory conversation with the stakeholders and an activist non-profit would reveal as being important to the business. These relationships need to be created and sustained by CSR departments in conjunction with those naturally created by line managers around the world.

Managing Transparency

For companies to be real players in public debates, they need to be transparent about their motives and how they live by their values. Growing pressure from society for companies to be much more explicit about their economic, social and environmental impacts has been welcomed by some companies. Shell, for example, has done an excellent job over the years in responding to powerful criticism by being much more open and engaging with its critics. It has taken the chance to thoughtfully explain how it functions in society, what its impact is and how it tries to manage major issues and the many dilemmas that it has to face.

Leading companies want to win a greater understanding and acceptance from society and public relations campaigns just don't cut it – a much more substantial and considered response is required. Company annual reports don't help either. A key job for a CSR or sustainability department is to help to develop and manage this new level of transparency and part of that is to produce social responsibility and sustainability reports of various kinds for the company. A company needs to articulate an integrated overview of its impact on society and its role as a corporate citizen, and while individual managers will play key roles in that process, it needs to be presented in a coherent form to external audiences right around the world and that is not something line managers can do.

One of the unintended effects of the development of sustainability and social responsibility reporting has been internal to the business. It has forced companies to identify issues, collect relevant data and they may then develop a policy in response. If there is no data available then the issues are not being actively managed and that in itself is a risk for the business. In my experience, company employees, including senior executives, are often surprised by their own CSR reports, where for the first time they get a comprehensive overview of the company's place in society. As a result, they can also feel better connected to the business, proud of its contribution to society beyond making the annual profit and know that difficulties are being actively managed.

Managing transparency is not just about sustainability reports and they have a limited value beyond specialist audiences. The truth is, they are not widely read but then neither are company financial reports. There is pressure on companies to produce integrated financial and sustainability reports, in part to give the subject status and as a symbol that the topic is integrated into the business. However, financial reports are legal documents and companies can be sued by investors if they bought/sold based on a report that was not accurate. Consequently, the accountants and lawyers are all over them and they are desperately risk averse, and integrated reports are not necessarily a good way to promote a dialogue with society about difficult issues. Companies need to have the freedom to be genuinely transparent about failings and dilemmas if they are to effectively address them. Openness about real issues and dilemmas is vital to developing dialogue and the trust that collaboration requires.

In practical terms, promoting genuine transparency in this day and age of electronic media is much easier than even 20 years ago. Issue papers and statements can be posted on websites and questions from stakeholders and the public answered almost immediately. CSR departments can make a big contribution to managing these communications. They have to be conducted in an 'adult' spirit with honesty and openness so that stakeholders and the wider public can see how the company is dealing with the realities of life in a global society and environment. It is tempting for companies to be defensive and want to control data and burnish their laurels all the time, but everyone knows that is not how life is. We all make mistakes and so often difficult choices are between two goods, not simple rights and wrongs.

Working With Others

Another area of where companies need to strengthen their internal skills and capacity is their ability to work with others on issues of concern. While line managers will have a vital role in addressing issues of concern to their particular function, like HR or supply chain, there are real skills to be used in developing partnerships with others that are beyond business skills. Having a specialist 'foreign affairs' unit that can develop these skills is a critical issue, given how this book has characterised the growing shape of global society. Collaboration across the formal sectors doesn't just happen; it is hard work and needs to be carefully managed.

One of the first things for companies to recognise is that many issues of concern are often related to products and practices of their whole industry, not single brands and individual companies, and these issues have to be tackled collectively by the industry. Consequently, the first group for companies to work with on social and environmental problems are other companies in the same industry or with the same problems. This is already happening in some industries and it is a positive thing.

The alcoholic drinks industry, for example, has long had to deal with the issue of the abuse of its products and has responded collectively as an industry. Despite differences in the types of drinks produced, and the fact that they are often in fierce competition, a wide group of drinks producing companies in the West and Japan have come together to form the International Alliance for Responsible Drinking (IARD), led by the CEOs of the member companies.[107] The issue of alcohol abuse is not one of brand or a particular type of drink – alcohol is in all of their products be they wine, beer or spirits – it is a generic problem for all producers. They have taken the initiative to come together in this and other ways to address the issue. Commercial retailers of various sorts from pubs and bars to supermarkets, are also involved in the issue particularly in respect of underage drinking but it is the producers that have taken the lead on the issue.

The producers of alcoholic drinks and IARD also work with others in society, including national governments and the UN Global Compact and responsible drinking organisations in countries around the world, where they try and address the issues such as the content of advertising, underage drinking and drink-driving. Furthermore, the organisation has negotiated The Dublin Principles with public health workers and the academic community in order to be transparent about business self-interest in funding the research that may be necessary to address the problem.[108] To help this engagement, several of the large drinks companies have specialist 'social aspects' managers who, like generic CSR managers, focus on the business/society interface. They bring the specialist knowledge and engagement skills necessary to confront a complex social problem that has a history going back to early Mesopotamia.

It is also important to note that despite the willingness of the industry to come forward and engage on the issues, there are many in the non-profit and public health community that are opposed to commercial companies being engaged in addressing alcohol issues. Their commercial and profit-making interest in producing alcoholic drinks is seen to disqualify them from having anything to say about the problems society faces. This view ignores the fact the both the Russian and Chinese governments, two of the largest drinks producers in the world, have seats on the Board of the World Health Organization (WHO) and are key to shaping its policies.

Companies do have their own interests, and there are many apparent conflicts of interest with the public health community, but companies also know a huge amount about how alcohol is consumed around the world. For elements of the public health community and key non-profits to refuse to engage with them is unproductive and this negative response can happen in many fields not just alcohol; the world does not give an unqualified welcome to corporate engagement.

As with the alcoholic drinks industry, an Industry-driven citizenship initiative transcends immediate company self-interest and tries to make a whole industry-wide contribution to an issue, which is important to the industry not just one company. These initiatives are different in character from trade associations, which have a primary role in promoting the business interests of member companies. Consequently, as an expression of good citizenship, companies have been part of creating organisations such as Roundtable on Sustainable Palm Oil (RSPO) founded in 2004, the Marine Stewardship Council and the Cocoa Foundation. These are multi-stakeholder organisations where the companies and non-profits sit down together to develop and implement policies on issues of mutual concern. The non-profits bring their expertise to the table and act as the guarantor of the public good in respect of the activities of the organisations, which have a key role in setting and spreading industry standards.

As it has contracted in scale, government has begun to reach out more to business for direct voluntary involvement in public issues. It has many agendas to fulfil and often needs additional resources and expertise from companies to achieve them. Business is not averse to working directly with government, but it has to be careful not to be drawn into every politically pressing issue at the bidding of a rotating group of politicians under pressure from the media. The type of long-term, carefully focused, commitment that IBM has had in the USA on education is a model of a positive contribution by a thoughtful corporate citizen.[109] It is a systems-based approach with a long-term perspective, not a short-term project, and is a performance-driven commitment using company cash, people and equipment to add measurable value to a public system of education.

Non-profits are also increasingly working directly with companies to address issues. These partnerships can be very close to their core business interests, such as a long-term and substantial focus on issues in the supply chain like sustainable fish and palm oil. They can also be far removed from the direct interest of the business, such as FedEx and Diageo's highly organised contributions to relief agencies when disasters happen. Either way, non-profits, like government, are increasingly willing and able to partner with companies. They want and need to access the vast resources and skills of the private sector, and as global corporate citizens.

On the other hand, companies are looking for credible partners to work with on their issues and a marketplace of bids and offers for corporate engagement is developing. In this marketplace for partnerships, some offers will be beyond what companies can reasonably do and must be turned down. Some non-profits are very choosy about what companies they will work with.

In addition to working with others in the government and non-profit sectors, companies can engage directly with ordinary people in the informal sector, particularly consumers, and this type of direct engagement has great potential. Consumer-facing companies have a tremendous reach into society and can partner with their customers to shape attitudes on issues such as recycling. Early examples of this engagement with consumers are Unilever using product 'care lines' to identify concerns about the use of washing powder. The overuse of detergent powder was costing the consumer money as well as being bad for the environment, and its brand Persil subsequently developed and marketed tablets of the right dose for a particular wash.

Texaco ran a consumer campaign in the UK called 'Children Should be Seen and Not Hurt' that provided high visibility armbands and other materials at service stations to help motorists see kids in the dark, which had a measurable impact on road accident rates.[110] The power and skill of corporate advertising to influence public attitudes and behaviour is potentially immense. Companies can also offer incentives for good behaviour, as Apple does today when it offers a trade-in discount to customers when they return their existing product for recycling prior to a new purchase.

There is a specialist craft in creating and maintaining the ability of companies to work with each other, with government, non-profits, consumers and the wider society, and it needs developing. Line managers are often too narrowly focused on their role and mostly too busy to get engaged beyond a certain point, and some partnerships have very intensive workloads. These are key reasons why there is more professionalism in the field of corporate responsibility management, just as in the past, managers grew to depend on HR professionals and ceased to try and do the whole job themselves.

In the past 30 years or so, the greatest progress in professionalising the field has been in environmental matters. They are often science-based – the answers to problems can often be clearly identified and progress towards solutions is measurable – and consequently environmental management fits well into a numbers-driven corporate culture. Economic and social issues remain complex and challenging, with different views about what is the right answer to problems; even if there is agreement on what the problem is. It is in the economic and social areas of corporate life that specialist staff working with senior managers and others in the company, can help develop a business's position on the issues and develop the responses it can make.

A company needs to be able to say what it thinks about an issue and what it feels as a company it can do as an individual corporate citizen. It then needs to be able to say what it can do in partnership with others such as non-profits and government, and what others need to do to address an issue. Companies cannot do everything and it is important for them to be clear about what it is they can and will do on any given issue. This sort of clarity makes it much easier to develop partnerships and for companies to play a part in responding to issues. If companies don't do the research and set their own agenda, they will constantly be pressed to work on other people's agendas.

Top-down or Bottom-up?

The CEOs of major companies are important players in public debates about society's issues, whether they like it or not. As a result of their position they will engage with a variety of 'global stakeholders' but of a somewhat different kind from those that country and frontline managers and employees will encounter. These stakeholders look to being consulted by companies on issues that concern them and want to lobby for their point of view, but they are not stakeholders in the sense that their lives are connected directly to the company and its operations. They are in fact important global opinion formers from the other two formal sectors and, like CEOs, they are invited to Davos, UN meetings and other global gatherings to debate the great issues of the day.

CEOs take part in these discussions and so they should as this is their distinct audience, one which no one else in the company can effectively engage with. This engagement is a positive development, which has evolved rapidly because business is no longer sidelined as it was in the Cold War, and business is now being drawn into debates about how to respond to global issues. It is blindingly obvious that global companies must be involved, since they are at the heart of the global economy, but it has taken a while for this reality to be acknowledged and we are only just working out how such engagement can be fully effected. However, there is a real danger in believing that these global debates and policies are the solution to society's problems – they are not, they are only one part of the solution.

Bottom-up innovation from employees in business functions in operating companies overseas and in specialist corporate responsibility units is every bit as important as top-down policy debates. We are trying to build a new and sustained discipline of managing corporate responsibility and sustainability in depth and few non-profits realise that. In his book *Connect: How Companies Succeed by Engaging Radically With Society*,[111] John Browne quotes global 'stakeholders' Amory Lovins, co-founder and chief scientist of the Rocky Mountain Institute, and Fred Krupp of the Environmental Defense Fund saying that they rarely work with CSR departments and insist on working with CEOs and corporate boards. They are convinced that they must work with the top people in order to get real change. Fred Krupp says:

> "Normally, the CSR function is a ghetto that's been established for PR reasons, promoting tiny contributions – vaccines they've donated, say, or playgrounds they've built – but ignoring the impact of the day-to-day business. We have not seen big change driven through partnerships with CSR officials so we have insisted in our work with companies that we meet with the CEO."

John Browne agrees with their view and goes on to dismiss the approach to CSR that companies have developed since the 1980s. He pretty much defines it as corporate community relations and 'environmental, social governance' (ESG) and says:

> "It is a small, uninspiring answer to a problem that requires a big picture solution. Inside business, executives view CSR as a fluffy, largely irrelevant cost centre. For civil society groups, it is meaningless propaganda that fails to achieve their goals. Neither side is satisfied. As one of the earliest CEO proponents of CSR, I feel well-placed to call for its final demise."

It is right to say that a company will do best in corporate responsibility and sustainability if the CEO and the board are fully informed and active because they will make the really big decisions. At the global level, the UN agreement on CFCs to save the ozone layer was a real success, and companies played a vital part in turning that issue around, along with governments, independent scientists and non-profit activists. It is a model for the type of engagement that is being argued here and points the way to the future. However, it is an unusual success not the norm and we still need much better collaboration between the sectors at the global level on issues such as climate change, plastic waste, poverty alleviation, access to medicines, mass migration and the whole SDG agenda.

In responding to the SDGs for example, it is wrong to underestimate the good that billions of dollars' worth of vaccines donated by major pharmaceutical companies does for millions of people around the world. About half of the healthcare commodities available in low-income countries are made available by donors and non-profits supported by major companies.[112] It is a mistake to make an urgent need for greater engagement by business an either/or situation between top leadership and CSR units, and it is the bottom-up approach driven by the real needs of actual stakeholders on the ground that provides much of the innovation to drive corporate citizenship forward. Having worked in a corporate CSR unit and consulted with many, they are so often the grit in the oyster that helps, in conjunction with managers and others, to produce the pearls of progress.

It is the job of a modern corporate CEO is to articulate the values of the company as it pursues its commercial business mission but they don't know everything, and they cannot be everywhere in the world all the time; they have a business to run. The CEO's second job is to build the internal capacities of the company to make sure those values are lived out right across the business and around the world. This necessarily involves animating managers and employees to reach out beyond the company to all its stakeholders and the wider society. An inspired corporate leader on the global stage is to be welcomed.

However, it is so often the vision and action of country, supply chain, marketing and production managers, together with their employee colleagues and CSR unit managers that need to be harnessed to develop global corporate citizenship strategies for the company. Millions of highly educated and effective people work for modern companies and they should all have a role in shaping their global citizenship agenda.

CHAPTER 9:

Corporate Citizenship and the Future of Capitalism

Capitalism Is Back

This book began with a reference to the earliest recorded examples of private enterprise and multinational businesses set up in ancient Assyria in 2000 BC, and also pointed out that a wider range of Mesopotamian societies had experimented over time with both free market and state control systems for managing the economy. It is an issue that greatly vexed humanity in the 19th and 20th centuries and with the collapse of communism, a period of history where humanity has experimented with a form of society that does not have private enterprise has come to an end. Capitalism is back for the next couple of generations at least, and this chapter looks at the role of corporate citizenship in its developing future.

As we look forward over the next millennium, the question is still 'what is the future of capitalism now?' The short answer is that we don't know and this book does not even try to answer the question. What we do know is that in the past 40 years or so a huge number of new private firms have been created and more are coming into being all the time, not least in the former socialist countries, but all round the world. As they enter the economy, how they view their role in society and their sense of responsibility towards it is an issue of considerable importance.

In some ways echoing Schumpeter's thoughts about the 'creative destruction' of capitalism, Michael L. Rothschild says in his book *Bionomics: The Inevitability of Capitalism:*[113]

"Capitalism, or market economy, or the free enterprise system – whatever you choose to label it – was not planned. Like life on Earth, it did not need to be. Capitalism just happened, and it will keep on happening. Quite spontaneously. Capitalism flourishes whenever it is not suppressed, because it is a naturally occurring phenomenon. It is the way human society organizes itself for survival in a world of limited resources.

"A capitalist economy can best be comprehended as a living ecosystem. Key phenomena observed in nature – competition, specialization, co-operation, exploitation, learning, growth, and several others – are also central to business life. Moreover, the evolution of the global ecosystem and the emergence of modern industrial society are studded with striking parallels."

Rothschild is right to point out the 'organic' nature of the capitalist system. Like trees in the forest, companies compete for space and live and die according to their capacities for growth and innovation. When one dies another takes its place and some become big and successful like Microsoft, which has the ability to stunt the growth of others. Companies exist in many forms of society today and some are autocratic and authoritarian. However, in a liberal capitalist economy, they co-exist with the rule of law, a free press, equality of religion, equality at the ballot box and free consumer choice. Large and small, they are now taken for granted as part of the social mix of a healthy modern society.

The immense creativity and power of these institutions has many downsides when seen as part of the social whole, and the future of the capitalist system as a whole will not be determined by good corporate citizenship. There are many broad ranging economic, social and environmental issues which will have a much more important effect on the future of the free market system and its companies. They can range from economic nationalism and trade wars, another global debt crisis, to mass unemployment and climate change, not to mention war and revolutions. All of which society has experienced before.

However, this book does not seek to engage in the debate about the broad macroeconomic impacts of the private enterprise system. They are fully debated elsewhere. It is focused on the role of the individual company as the agent of the market economy and how it should behave in society. Companies exist, therefore we need to have a theory about how they should function as citizens of society as well as commercial entities. This approach is not an answer to society's great challenges but a contribution to helping address them. Companies have to step forward and use their resources and skills to play a constructive part in solving them. Their chances of being an acceptable part of society are somewhat increased if the millions of people who work for them every day all around the world believe that their company is not just about making a profit but seeking to act as a force for good in society.

The strength of this approach is that it seeks to give guidance to business leaders, managers and employees when making decisions about the role of their company within local, national and international society. Whatever the debates raging on around them about the legal status of the company, economic justice, the impacts of globalisation and mass consumption, decision-makers in business have to live their daily lives in a constructive way. They need to make good business choices and try to make good decisions about the great issues of our time as they manifest themselves for the business. The wider society will be constantly debating and changing the capitalist system in which a company operates, but while this debate goes on, those companies as citizens of society, need to be empowered to make the best decisions they can.

Capitalism and Good Citizenship

However, companies also exist within the free market framework of modern capitalism. This is the context that constrains and directs them, and they, like society in general, cannot ignore it. An absolutely central one, the price we pay for free enterprise, is massive economic inequality, which has grown in a very stark way in former socialist countries like Russia and China. Since the early writings of Marx, the exploitation and wealth accumulation of the 'capitalist class' has elicited intense criticism and opposition. Many still use this argument as sufficient reason to control private companies and indeed eliminate them.

While not advocating such an approach, Oxfam's 2017 report *Reward Work Not Wealth*, confronts the issues and states that a CEO in the USA earns the same amount of money for about one day of work as an average worker makes in a year: and that corporate leaders Jeff Bezos, Bill Gates and Warren Buffet own as much wealth as the bottom 50% of the US population – about 160 million people.[114] Oxfam argues that in order to end extreme poverty society must also end extreme wealth, and while Bill Gates and Warren Buffet can point to their massive commitment to personal philanthropy as their response to this argument, companies still have to deal with issues like executive pay and bonuses. As the future develops will they stick to the script and say that these salaries are inevitable or will they do something about them? They have the power to, but will they use it?

Many other issues in a free market economy impact on the ability of companies to be good corporate citizens but three such issues stand out as having special significance for this discussion, because they potentially constrain good corporate citizenship but in some cases offer opportunities to exercise it.

First among them is the power of shareholders who can, and have, occasionally acted on issues like executive pay. However, the short-term profit maximising undertaken by certain sections of the investor community and the asset stripping approach that others use is a major problem for individual companies. While I have previously argued that most companies in the real economy of providing goods and services are in reality, long-term profit optimisers not short-term maximisers, that is not true of the free market system as a whole. Shareholders as owners may well have other agendas, so do want to maximise the value of their shares and good corporate citizenship is no reason not to.

Unilever is often cited as an example of a good corporate citizen, and recently it was the victim of a hostile takeover bid by Kraft Heinz, 50% of which is owned by US group 3G Capital and Warren Buffet. At the time, the pound was at a low against the dollar and British companies looked cheap to buy, and among existing shareholders there those who were pressing the CEO Paul Polman to sell out and maximise the value of their Unilever shares. Commenting on the failure of the bid, the City Editor of the *London Evening Standard*, Jim Armitage, a staunch defender of free market policies, said on 1st March 2017:[115]

"Chat to fund managers and bosses since the 3G bid and you'll invariably hear them pronounce on how Unilever boss Paul Polman's biggest mistake has been his obsession with sustainability, ethics and the environment. Forget the greenwash, they chime and focus on the bottom line.

"What infuriating tosh. Hasn't the rise of anti-business populism in the West taught these people anything? Multinationals that treat their workforce well, invest in their business, and don't trash the regions they operate in are what we need, not what we want to destroy.

"Unilever has a decent record of retaining operations in the UK, insourcing rather than outsourcing jobs and investing in its brands and businesses. 3G, or some other debt-fuelled fast buck merchants, could quickly and easily rip up those long-term strategies for a short, sharp boost to profit margins. But that would derail the longer-term gains Unilever's actions have brought its investors over the years; 8% annual dividend growth over 36 years for one.

"Its reputation as a decent corporate citizen is cited by 51% of its graduate intake and has given it industry leading staff retention, with 91% of employees saying they're proud to work there.

"Let's deal with this nonsense that Polman's policies have been bad for profits. Unilever's investment in core brands (£23bn since 2009), has created more spin-offs and product innovations than rivals, making its goods more desirable to customers.

"This means it can charge an average of 20% premium above the competition and drive up profitability for the long-term."

This strong defence of Paul Polman and Unilever supports my view that socially responsible behaviour by good corporate citizens is not only possible but can make real business sense in terms of the bottom line. However, it also shows how such corporate citizenship is at risk from short-term profit maximising in the stock market. That is a fact of the capitalist system and while I don't join that debate here, I heartily approve of Jim Armitage's views.

Some investors are short-term in their approach, driven by quarterly numbers. They are a bit like the bomber force: they fly at 40,000 feet above the daily conflict of business life and don't see first-hand the damage to human lives that their decisions make. On the other hand, the folk at Unilever and indeed at most companies on the frontline of life, are the foot soldiers of the competitive marketplace and they know only too well what impact their decisions can have on the lives of ordinary people. To improve profitability, they may well have to shut a plant or cut off long-term suppliers and these are tough, often very personal decisions for managers to make and implement. They have to face a wide range of ethical dilemmas and, as managers and ordinary human beings, they have moral sentiments that affect their decision-making. For them it is a real face-to-face situation, not a purely numbers based and short-term economic analysis.

Second, is one of the many other 'systemic' issues that arise within the global free market system that this book doesn't address, is the question of global responsibility in taxation. Society's big decision is to allow companies to be created and operate and they are new to many such societies like China. Once a company exists, it is part of society and paying its taxes is the membership fee it pays to be in the club, just like an individual citizen. Paying the company's fairly assessed burden of taxes is a primary responsibility for business just as it is for individuals. Taxes are part of the price we have to pay as businesses and individuals for having a society worth living in, and anyone who cheats has no right to be called a 'good' citizen whatever else they do. If a company cheats on its taxes, then whatever it does in respect of good corporate citizenship will be suspect and lack credibility.

The campaigning group UK Uncut among others has accused companies including Topshop and Starbucks of being engaged in highly manipulative tax avoidance schemes because of the way international jurisdictions allow international companies to move money around the world. The choice to exploit loopholes and other opportunities in international tax law is open to many big companies. When the owners and leaders of these companies get rich by these means and other strategies such as offshoring and zero-hours contracts, they actively promote massive economic inequality. These decisions are damaging and fuel a profound hostility to business in society.

These broad issues will have to be dealt with both at the level of global society and through law and regulation but also by a degree of self-regulation by individual companies as they develop their tax policies. While there are systemic pressures within the capitalist/free market system from shareholders and others that drive many corporate decisions, such as the use of tax havens (facilitated by advice from clever accountants and lawyers), companies can also take into account other ethical and citizenship factors if they have the values and commitment to do so. Like individual citizens, companies have to choose how to behave in respect of paying their taxes; they just have more tempting options to avoid and evade them.

Third is the continuing problem of the 'external diseconomies' that business activities impose on society and the environment. These diseconomies are easy for companies to ignore and many do. Not least because there is often a financial price to be paid for addressing them and companies don't want to pick up the costs. However, with a little thought and effort they can be turned into opportunities to demonstrate good corporate citizenship and may even help the commercial success of the business.

There could be major concerns such as carbon pollution, which requires massive economy-wide action by all businesses, or small but irritating issues of waste, such as chewing gum being discarded in public areas. Individual companies can act on carbon pollution and should, but the answer requires a large-scale response involving all forms of business – and soon. However, a single issue like chewing gum pollution which connects directly to the business of one or two companies, is a good opportunity for those companies to demonstrate leadership and good corporate citizenship. We know it costs the consumer about 30 pence to buy a piece of chewing gum and local government about £1.50 to clean it up when it is dropped on the pavement.[116]

When a company such as Wrigley has about 90% of the UK market, what is it going to do about the situation? I am not suggesting that the company has the whole solution to these problems but I would say that they have to be involved in developing a response. There is a self-interest in their doing so because they will want to protect their 'licence to operate', but they should also have some good ideas to offer. Wrigley launched a 'Bin It for Good' campaign but has yet to be persuaded to switch to biodegradable raw materials, and it could see a competitor taking the lead if it did so. Lego, which is one of the world's great producers of small bits of plastic, has seen the writing on the wall for plastic pollution in society and the ocean and has invested in creating a botanicals range made from ethanol fermented from sugar. It has set demanding targets to reduce the use of oil-based plastic by 2030 and has done so without legislation – this is an example of good citizenship in action.[117]

Companies Need Manageable Priorities

Companies cannot do everything and they need to be open about constraints and clear about what they as an individual business can do on issues that they see as important. They also need to know what they can do in partnership with others such as non-profits and government, and also what others such as individual consumers or governments need to do. One of the major disincentives for companies to systematically engage with society on the issues is that they tend to see such engagement as a 'slippery slope', with no clear end point in sight. They will say: "We are not a charity, you know", and that is true. To avoid this problem, companies need to be clear about the limits of their engagement and have the courage to assert them, be that in respect of working with the community at a small plant, or on a major global issue such as climate change.

The intellectual effort involved in mapping an exposure to the issues is well worth the investment of management time and a key way to set boundaries for a company's engagement with society. There are several ways to do this and active stakeholder engagement is really valuable. Companies have published examples of their ranking of issues in sustainability reports and this lets stakeholders and society know how the company sees its role in society and what its priority issues are.

A company may well work on all of these, but from this process a few key issues may emerge as key priorities. A map can be developed for pretty much any company and it is from this that the company can define its priorities and articulate them to the wider society. Not everyone may agree with the order of priorities, but at least there is a clear basis for a discussion of what the company's priorities for social and environmental responsibility are.

A further advantage to mapping is the way in which it enables managers and employees to know what the company's priority issues are. Managers and employees around the world can then align with them as priorities and consequently clear boundaries are set for corporate engagement and action. However, each of the different functions – supply chain, manufacturing, distribution, and sales and marketing – within the company, will have their own special economic, social and environmental factors to consider, as will country managers. Multinationals in particular operate in diverse cultures with specific issues such as religious prohibitions on certain ingredients in food and products that their senior executives may not even be aware of. In addition to mapping out corporate priority issues, country managers and functional managers need to be empowered to take on local issues too; local and functional flexibility is essential.

I once sat in a Heathrow hotel for nearly three days with Unilever supply chain managers for the Home and Personal Care side of the company. We went through every single item that was bought into the business and did an economic, social and environmental risk assessment for each of them. While the process was initiated by corporate headquarters, it was led entirely by the managers themselves. We used a matrix and reviewed everything from chemicals in soap powder, chalk for toothpaste and plastic bags for soap tablets that go into washing machines, to promotional items like hats and T-shirts. At the end of the exercise, these middle managers had generated their own supply chain managers' map of economic, social and environmental risk for all inputs into the Home and Personal Care business. They cross-referred their findings to the company Code of Business Principles and prioritised key risks for immediate action and others for longer-term concern.

There may still have been issues that we missed in the process, and this is where the work of local and international non-profits comes in. They often pick up on issues that company managers just don't see because they are not as close to the localities that feed into these massive supply chains. Good practice in priority setting today requires companies to find credible independent third parties and get them to contribute their ideas. The work done by many companies to organise systematic stakeholder engagement programmes and set up dialogues with non-profits and community experts has been really helpful in this respect. The process generates insights for the company into its evolving relations with society but also exposes non-profits and others to the company's approach to doing business and the dilemmas it faces.

This approach works with the single business units of large companies too, and in that respect can be transferred to the operations of any small business. For example, while working for the International Finance Corporation (IFC) in Kenya, I was involved in applying this type of analysis to the Serena Hotel in Nairobi, which is part of the wider Serena Group. It was a well-run business within the local market and took the Group's values seriously. Great care was taken in the quality of its service and considerable effort was spent on ensuring food quality and good hygiene, for example. Consequently, it was a small extension of the management approach of the business generally, to address issues such as child labour in the production and delivery of food, as well as in ancillary services such as car cleaning. Managers actively manage value chains in terms of quality, price and delivery and it is not a huge development to include wider economic, social and environmental concerns into this approach.

In the future, not only will private firms need to be clear about the focus of their social and environmental responsibilities and challenges, but they will have to have a strategy to educate employees about them and empower them to act on them. The capitalism of the future may be like the past in many ways but it needs to embrace an added dimension of social and environmental awareness and act on it. All managers and employees need to be educated and trained to support the company's citizenship strategy as they undertake their traditional business roles and as individual citizens. This is something they can do to help make the world a better place and take pride in doing so.

Having been involved in such training with supply chain managers for companies including Cadbury, Unilever and Vodafone, managers learn quickly and will take on the challenge. They are living the dynamic of modern capitalism and know that a simple 'business' decision to change a metal box supplier from the north of England to a factory in China may make commercial sense but it can seriously affect people's lives. There would be the issues of human rights to be faced in Chinese manufacturing and unemployed workers in an old metalworking community in the UK. It is just not reasonable to ask purchasing managers to know all there is to know about all these issues, and as was argued in the preceding chapter, they need help and support to manage them internally from CSR units as well as externally. The same point is true for managers in every corporate function from HR to marketing and distribution.

Modern capitalism functions in a much more open and democratic society than in the past, one with undreamed-of connectivity, one where employees are better educated than in the past. Even so, when operating at a local, national and international level, companies cannot be experts in everything, but there are people in the community who are closer to the problem and managers need to be able to make use of them. If we are to make our new tripartite system of global 'governance' work, then the three formal sectors need to be able to call on each other to help address issues that affect society and the environment, at whatever level in the company is the most appropriate, not just at the level of the executive office. Its job is to give focus to the company's social and environmental responsibility and empower employees to live it out in an organic and creative way.

Companies as a Force for Good

Many in society remain hostile to the private sector and focus exclusively on the large-scale problems associated with its activities. They are real concerns, but companies contain within them great potential for fostering positive change, as part of, and alongside their commercial activities. If companies have the values and capacity to contribute to society's development, they will not only be known for the goods and services they provide but for their contribution as citizens too. They need to embrace this role fully as we move into a new generation of a capitalist society and articulate exactly what their citizenship commitments are. We need to blur the distinctions between the three formal sectors and see companies as a force for good as well as non-profits and government. The other sectors in turn need to see that they are often in business themselves and have many close links with the private sector.

Politicians, governments and non-profits need to get real about the power of private firms and the role they play in our global society. They need a much more thoughtful approach and be willing to engage with the private companies of the world. After all, they have many aspects of creativity and power that the other two organised sectors don't have. Private sector companies exist because they are good at meeting many of people's wants and needs and much of its activity is life-enhancing. Above all, private firms are good with money in a way that many governments and non-profits are often not, and that fact raises some intriguing possibilities.

The private sector runs on supply and demand, the exchange of money for goods and services, and this apparent rationality can lull it into a state of profitable complacency. When buying and selling, private firms use money to create a huge part of our social reality. As Yuval Noah Harari says in his book *Sapiens: A Brief History of Humankind*:[118]

> "For thousands of years, philosophers, thinkers and prophets have besmirched money and called it the root of all evil. Be that as it may, money is also the apogee of human tolerance. Money is more open-minded than language, state laws, cultural codes, religious beliefs and social habits. Money is the only trust system created by humans that can bridge almost any cultural gap, and that does not discriminate on the basis of religion, gender, race, age or sexual orientation. Thanks to money, even people who don't know each other and don't trust each other can nevertheless cooperate effectively."

Harari makes a point that is very little discussed in business's relations with society, the way in which they try to treat customers around the world the same. Furthermore, this outlook is how small-scale Muslim farmers in sub-Saharan Africa can put food on the family table of wealthy Christian Europeans – they get paid for doing so. Consequently, there is an important relationship managed by companies that potentially could be developed to be much more than simply an economic one. Coffee companies like Starbucks and Costa understand this and are seeking to link their customers to the suppliers of their customers' drinks. Can such relationships be the basis of a wider understanding and collaboration around the world if they are consciously developed as such? The Fair Trade movement has been trying to do this, because when money changes hands, people engage and can have a strong incentive to treat one another fairly.

I learned about the power of such financial incentives to change attitudes when learning about how Levi's integrated its Blackstone plant in Virginia in the 1950s. The company only lost one employee, who quit at her husband's insistence. The rest stayed because Levi's gave them all, black and white, good wages and benefits that helped greatly with family life. After the integration, Ed Cray says in his book *Levi's:*[119]

> "Initially, blacks and whites avoided each other on the job. In a week they were eating together in the plant cafeteria. Blackstone was quietly integrated."

White workers had the financial incentive, which only the company could provide, to overcome their prejudice in favour of a better life for themselves and their black neighbours. It was a sad day when the plant closed, but the local paper ran an editorial which said how much the community had benefited economically from the investment Levi's had brought and that the company had helped the community learn to live together. The company integrated all its plants in due course and never once had a dispute. The process was done with sensitivity based on a careful combination of both social responsibility and straightforward business concerns for a stable supply of productive workers.

This is not an argument to say trade and business necessarily promotes peace and understanding, as there are too many cases of it doing the opposite. What Harari also says is that we know money has a dark side too and it can corrupt human values, intimate relations and the politics of whole nations:

> "It is common nowadays to believe that the market always prevails, and that the dams erected by kings, priests and communities cannot long hold back the tides of money. This is naïve. Brutal warriors, religious fanatics and concerned citizens have repeatedly managed to trounce calculating merchants and even to reshape the economy."

This is the challenge to business: can it, through the adoption of values and creative citizenship policies, use its economic power for the greater good? Just as business can change employee attitudes, it can also change those of suppliers, communities, consumers and perhaps even investors too. The imposition of new national and international laws may well be part of changing business behaviour but it cannot force companies to adopt a wider role in society. That has to come by choice and it will be company by company. Companies need to be ready and able to pick up a role as a corporate citizen, which is special to them, one based on a clearly understood set of values that, in our interconnected world, is impossible to avoid. So, companies might as well get on with facing the challenge in a constructive way and in doing so, help to shape the future of the capitalist system.

Not all companies will, of course, and there will always be companies like Enron[120] that say all the right things about their values but are found to be living a fraud. For most companies 'business as usual' is the attractive option, but those that don't think like this can be very powerful in shaping the future of the capitalist economy and the wider global society. This is a particular challenge to those new companies that are rising fast in developing countries like China and India; I am concerned with what these vast new companies think their role is in society at home and increasingly abroad. If the Chinese and Indians want to continue to criticise the British East India Company and the capitalism of the past, which they are entitled to do, then their companies need to do a lot better today and thereby play a role in shaping the capitalism of the future.

Corporate Citizenship as Part of Shaping a New Future

Since the fall of the Berlin Wall in 1989, humanity has begun to create a global social system that has given the private sector a massive role in both economic and social life. It is now the driver of global economic growth, giving people the goods and services they want and need. Can humanity now recognise that we have begun to create an institutional structure that represents the way we humans consciously and unconsciously think and act? We are creating three formal sectors that can be seen to represent different aspects of the human mind and how it works in the public, as well as the private space. A key feature of psychological thinking is to help individuals integrate conflicted aspects of their minds and have them work together in harmony, often with the aim of avoiding a repeat of destructive patterns of behaviour. Can we apply this type of thinking to the three formal sectors of our emerging global society? I think we can to some degree, and should.

Furthermore, I think the private sector is the most difficult of the three formal sectors to integrate with the other two, partly because it is successful as it is. Companies need a new 'script' for the future, a script that leads them to step forward and take a role in engaging with society's concerns. It is no good just talking about the private sector in gross aggregate terms; it also needs to be understood at the level of the individual company, its mission, values and role in society, because corporations in all their diversity are key players in shaping our world. They live by the rules of the market, of which making a profit is central, but they are much more than profit-making machines. They are living human organisms and, like individual citizens, have a great potential for good and bad, just on a much larger scale.

I agree with John Browne and his collaborators from McKinsey who look at business and society relations from a CEO's perspective (mine is a middle manager's view), when they say in their book *Connect*:[121]

> "Fixing a relationship that has been intermittently dysfunctional for over 2,000 years will take some doing....
>
> "...If business wants a fundamentally different relationship with the external world, it needs to adopt an entirely new attitude. It needs to 'engage radically'. This means being far more open than in the past. It means meeting important stakeholders regularly and making friends before they are needed. And it means communicating to outsiders in clear language, without resorting to propaganda. Openness sounds simple but in fact it contradicts an inherent corporate preference for tight controls on the flow of information. Companies will never make peace with society as long as they treat stakeholders with the suspicion traditionally reserved for enemies."

Individual companies have always taken responsibility for their own wellbeing by making a profit, but the future requires them to know how to contribute to the common good in a systematic way. The modern world, with all its freedoms and opportunities for both individuals and institutions such as companies, also requires both individuals and corporate entities to live with a far greater sense of self-awareness and responsibility. The days of government doing everything for us are over and humanity is choosing a different form of society, one with a dynamic private sector. While that has given companies huge commercial opportunities, they have to articulate and act on the responsibilities that come with that new freedom if capitalism is to have a future that is in some degree different from the past.

Fortunately, humanity has also begun to articulate global standards of behaviour and values for our global society; they are an invaluable guide for business and the latest iteration is that of the SDGs. Companies need to pay regard to the SDGs and be conscious of their wide-ranging impacts, and then be clear about the contribution they can make to achieving them. They also need to be open to engagement and partnership with others in order to be able to address the problems that the SDGs have identified. Companies have great power and resources but they don't have all the answers and there are real limits to their power and resources. That is why the idea of partnerships with the other two formal sectors to address humanity's problems is essential.

At this point in history, we have an opportunity to make a new global social system work if we can consciously face up to what is required. A new general theory of business as a social and environmental force is needed, as is a theory of society based on the three formal sectors and the informal sector complementing and supporting each other across the whole range of human endeavour. These projects are for others to undertake. This book is just an extrapolation of historic and current trends to make the point that it is worth developing the concept of corporate citizenship as a modest contribution to the planet's future.

Notes and References

1   **Part 1: The Historical and Cultural Context**

    Introduction

    Robert Owen founded the textile mill communities of New Lanark in Scotland from 1800 and New Harmony in the USA from 1924. New Lanark was a "company town" with extensive social provision but New Harmony and other initiatives were not successful. He was an early example of an enlightened "capitalist" who saw that the route to making a profit did not necessarily require the exploitation of his workers.

2   Marx, Karl (1867) *Das Kapital: Critique of Political Economy*, in German: Verlag von Otto Meisner.

3   Marx, Karl and Engels, Friedrich (1948) *The Communist Manifesto* commissioned by the Communist League and published in London in 1848, the "year of revolutions".

4   Moore, Karl and Lewis, David (April 1998) The First Multinationals: Assyria circa 2000 BC, Management International Review.

Chapter 1: Private Companies Are Part of the Development of Human Culture

5   See 4, above.

6   Kriwaczek, Paul (2012) *Babylon: Mesopotamia and the Birth of Civilization*, London: Atlantic Books.

7   Browne, John, Nuttall, Robin and Stadlen, Tommy (2015) *Connect: How Companies Succeed By Engaging Radically With Society*, London: W.H. Allen.

8   Milton, Giles (1999) *Nathaniel's Nutmeg*, London: Hodder and Stoughton.

9   Lawson, Philip (1987) *The East India Company: A History*, London: Longman Studies in Modern History

10 Wikipedia gives a full account of how the British became one of the world's largest consumers of tea from the very earliest days of its importation.

11 Trentmann, Frank (2016) *Empire of Things: How We Became a World of Consumers, from the Fifteenth Century to the Twenty-First*, London: Allen Lane.

12 Engels was sent by his family to the Manchester branch of the family firm which was founded in Germany in 1844, the original factory there closed in 1979 as production was moved to Asia.

13 Marx and Engels along with others, were protesting against exploitation of workers by international capitalism and their extensive writings about class conflict became the basis for the major political movements of communism and socialism in the 19th and 20th centuries. The social and economic systems of countries like the Soviet Union and China were based on their ideas.

14 Lovell, Julia (2011) *The Opium War*, London: Picador

15 Berridge, Virginia (1981) *Opium and the People*, London: Free Association Books.

16 Hudson, Pat The Limits of Wool and the Potential of Cotton in the Eighteenth and Nineteenth Centuries http://www.lse.ac.uk/Economic-History/Assets/Documents/Research/GEHN/Helsinki/HELSINKIHudson.pdf: Cardiff University.

17 Rivoli, Pietra (2005) *The Travels of a T-shirt in the Global Economy*, Hoboken: John Wiley and Sons Inc.

18   The resistance to cheaply produced cotton cloth was central to the Indian independence struggle and the symbol of the spinning wheel, to ensure self-sufficiency in textiles, was widely adopted. The spinning wheel was replaced on the national flag by the wheel of Ashoka, when it was formally adopted at independence in 1947.

19   Robbins, Nick (2006) *The Corporation That Changed the World: How the East India Company Shaped the Modern Multinational*, London and Ann Arbor: Pluto Press.

20   This is a controversial period of history about which debate still rages but from the point of view of this book, it is the time when private firms, not government, began to re-emerge as major forces in shaping society around the world.

21   Tooze, Adam (2006) *The Wages of Destruction: The Making and Breaking of the Nazi Economy*, London: Penguin.

22   Welby, Justin (2016) *Dethroning Mammon: Making Money Serve Grace*, London: Bloomsbury.

23   Weber, Max (1930) *The Protestant Ethic and the Spirit of Capitalism*, London: Routledge.

24   Tawney, R. (1926) *Religion and the Rise of Capitalism*, New Brunswick: Transaction Publishers.

25   James, Harold (2006) *Family Capitalism: Wendels, Haniels, Falcks and the Continental European Model*, Cambridge Massachusetts: The Belknap Press of Harvard University Press.

26   Nicholson, Virginia (2002) *Among the Bohemians: Experiments in Living 1900 –1939*, London: Penguin.

27   To some extent this movement was started by Matthew Arnold in writings like Culture and Anarchy and was connected with a theme of anti-industrialisation associated with artists like William Morris.

28   Bradshaw, Tim (Jan 20th 2017) "Silicon Valley seeks ethical solutions to avert populist backlash over jobs threat", London: *Financial Times*.

29   Bridge, Mark (Wednesday Feb 15th 2017) "Musk backs basic income in robot future", London: *The Times*.

Chapter 2: The Resurgent For-Profit Sector

30   Shumpeter, Joseph (1943) *Capitalism, Socialism and Democracy*, Abingdon: Routledge.

31   Oxfam's Annual Report for 2016.

32   Wier, Christopher (1994) *Jesse Boot of Nottingham*, Nottingham: The Boots Company.

33   Lala, R. M. (1992) *Beyond The Last Blue Mountain: A Life of J.R.D Tata*, New Delhi: Penguin Books India.

34   Carnegie, Andrew (1920) Autobiography, New York: Signet Classics.

35   Cove, Peter (2017) *Poor No More: Rethinking Dependency and the War on Poverty*, New York: Routledge.

Chapter 3: The Rise of a Global Social System

36   General Government Spending Total, as % of GDP, 2016, Index of Economic Freedom.

37   Public and Private Sector Employment Data, 2013, ILO Statistics.

38   Hochschild, Adam (2005) *Bury the Chains: The British Struggle to Abolish Slavery*, New York: Houghton Mifflin.

39 May 29th 2018, *The Times* of London published a story documenting a report published in 2002, which identified 40 aid organisations where allegations had been made that staff were involved in sexually exploitative relations with refugee children, most were local organisations but 15 international organisations were also implicated.

40 The Founder and Director of New Era Philanthropy, John G Bennett Jnr was sentenced to 12 years in prison in 1997 for running a Ponzi scheme under the auspices of the charity.

41 Bill Aramony, the Chief Executive of United Way of America was sentenced in 1995 to six years in prison for defrauding the charity.

42 Salamon, Lester M. and Anheier, Helmut K. (1997) *Defining the Non-Profit Sector: A Cross-National Analysis*, Manchester England: Manchester University Press.

43 US Census Bureau statistics that give all government employees as 14,425,359 out of 121,490,000 employees in total in 2015.

44 ILO Statistics for 2013 (ILOSTAT) cites public sector employment at 12.1% of the total, and private sector employment as 87.9% of the total.

45 Carson, Rachel (1962) *Silent Spring*, New York: Houghton Mifflin.

46 The Universal Declaration of Human Rights was adopted by the UN General Assembly in 1948, and of the 58 members at the time 48 were in favour none against, two did not vote and eight abstained including the Soviet bloc countries. It was the first step towards the International Bill of Human Rights which came into force in 1976.

47 The Sustainable Development Goals replaced the Millennium Development Goals which ended in 2015. There are 17 goals set by the UN to address climate change, hunger, gender equality and environmental concerns. Companies have some role in shaping them and the goals touch on what they do as businesses. For example, goal 12 calls for responsible consumption and production and asks companies to promote sustainable practices and produce sustainability reports.

48 In January 1996, the Granada TV company's *World in Action* team aired a programme called St Michael: Has the Halo Slipped? suggesting that the company had knowingly sourced from a supplier that used child labour and was falsely labelling garments made in the UK when they were made in Morocco. The company won the ensuing libel case and *World in Action* paid £50,000 in damages and the legal costs.

49 Greyson, David (2013) *Silence is Not Golden: Golden Agri-Resources, Greenpeace and Sustainable Palm Oil*, Cranfield School of Management, ref No 713-039-1.

Chapter 4: The World Companies Now Live in

50 Unilever Sustainability Report (2017) Unilever is one of the few companies that publish a cash value added figure thus enabling an approximate comparison with country GDP figures.

51 Clay, Jason (2005) Exploring the Links Between International Business and Poverty Reduction: A Case Study of Unilever in Indonesia, Oxford: Oxfam UK.

52 The Global 500 List is published each year by *Fortune* Magazine, it is ranked on size by sales but also gives data on employees, profits and country of origin.

53 Hampden-Turner, Charles and Trompenaars, Alfons (1993) *The Seven Cultures of Capitalism*, New York: Doubleday. Hall, Peter A. and Soskice, David (2001) Varieties of Capitalism: the Institutional Foundations of Comparative, Advantage, Oxford: Oxford University Press.

54   Cray, Edward (1978) *Levi's: The "Shrink-to-Fit" business that stretched to cover the world*, Boston: Houghton Mifflin.

55   Rees, Sian (2010) *Sweet Water and Bitter: The Ships That Stopped The Slave Trade*, London: Vintage.

56   US Foreign Corrupt Practices Act 1977.

57   Salamon, Lester M. and Anheier, Helmut K. (1997) *Defining the Non-profit Sector: A Cross-National Analysis*, Manchester England: Manchester University Press.

58   Casey, John (2016) Comparing Nonprofit Sectors Around the World, Journal of Nonprofit Education and Leadership Vol. 6.

59   The Charitable Uses Act of 1601 passed at the time of Queen Elizabeth I laid the foundations of modern charitable law in the English-speaking world. It has been regularly updated and developed most notably in the 1993 Charities Act and again in the 2006 Charities Act as the role of charities in society grows and develops.

60   Lipset, Seymour Martin (1996) *American Exceptionalism: A Double-Edged Sword*, New York: W. W. Norton and Company.

61   Lipset, Seymour Martin (2000) *It Didn't Happen Here: Why Socialism Failed in the United States*, New York: W. W. Norton and Company.

62   Salamon, Lester M. and Sokolowski, S. Wojciech and List, Regina (2003) *Global Civil Society: An Overview*, Baltimore MD: Johns Hopkins University, Center for Civil Society Studies.

63   Oxfam Annual Report and Accounts for 2016/17.

64   Saunders, Cicley (2005) *Watch With Me: Inspiration for a Life in Hospice Care*, London: Observatory Publications.

65   Behr, Edward (1997) *Prohibition: The 13 Years That Changed America*, London: Penguin Books and BBC Books.

66   In 2001, the BBC gave coverage to a vessel called the MV Etirino found off the coast of West Africa taking about 40 children to work in cocoa farms in the region and the echo of an earlier slave trade was very real.

67   The Global Compact was launched in July 2000 with 10 principles to encourage business to adopt sustainable and socially responsible practices around the world. It has over 13,000 participants in 170 countries.

68   Hudson Institute (2013) *The Index of Global Philanthropy and Remittances*, New York: Hudson Institute.

Chapter 5: Working Together?

69   Browne, John, with Anderson, Philippa (2010) *Beyond Business: An Inspirational Memoir from a Remarkable Leader*, London: Weidenfeld and Nicolson.

70   Milton, Richard (2001) *Bad Company: Behind the Corporate Mask*, Thirsk: House of Stratus.

71   Berne, Eric, MD (1964) *Games People Play: The Psychology of Human Relationships*, London: Penguin Books.

72   Berne, Eric, MD (1964) *Games People Play: The Psychology of Human Relationships*, London: Penguin Books.

73   Steiner, Claude (1974) *Scripts People Live*, New York: Bantam Books.

74   http://www.ericberne.com/im-ok-youre-ok-by-thomas-a-harris/

75   Tindale, Stephen (2008) *Going Green: Straight Talk from the World's Top Business Leaders*, Lesson Ten, Boston: Fifty Lessons Limited.

Part 2 Introduction

76   Clotfelter, Charles (1985) *Charitable Giving and Tax Legislation in the Reagan Era*, Law and Contemporary Problems, USA.

77   The Conference Board and CECP (2016) Giving in Numbers 2017 Edition, New York: The Conference Board.

78   Elkington, John (1987) *Cannibals With Forks: The Triple Bottom Line of 21st Century Business*, Oxford: Capstone Publishing.

Chapter 6: What is Corporate Citizenship?

79   Bakan, Joel (2004) *The Corporation: The Pathological Pursuit of Profit and Power*, London: Constable and Robinson.

80   Greenfield, Kent (2006) *The Failure of Corporate Law: Fundamental Flaws and Progressive Possibilities*, Chicago: University of Chicago Press.

81   "B" Corporations are certified by an international non-profit organisation that promotes the idea around the world. There are more than 500 such companies and their status is recognised in more than 30 US states. Patagonia became the first such company in California in 2012.

82   Diageo Foundation (2017) 25 Year Impact Report, London Diageo.

Chapter 7: Why Be a Good Citizen?

83   Roddick, Anita (1991) *Body and Soul*, London: Ebury Press.

84   While working for Cadbury in Ghana, I stayed in the company guest house in Kumasi where I found and read a hand-typed book detailing the history of the company in the country and the role it played in developing cocoa growing in Ghana. Part of the account was a discussion of the payment of a premium of up to 10% of the market price to farmers who dried their crops off the ground to ensure quality and freedom from contamination. I have no idea if this vital document was ever saved in the Cadbury archives as the property was subsequently sold off.

85   Macqueen, Adam (2004) *The King of Sunlight: How William Lever Cleaned Up the World*, London: Bantam Press.

86   Unilever PLC London published the study which mapped claims against purchasing decisions.

87   Global Tolerance (2016) The Values Revolution, London.

88   The Global Sustainable Investment Review is the third in a series since 2012 and is published by the Global Sustainable Investment Alliance, a membership based organisation of sustainable investment organisations around the world.

89   Grayson, David and Hodges, Adrian (2004) *Corporate Social Opportunity: 7 Steps to Make Social Responsibility Work for Your Business*, London: Blackwell's.

90   Drucker, Peter (Winter 1984) The New Meaning of Corporate Social Responsibility, California Management Review, vol xxvi

91   Porter, Michael E. and Kramer, Mark R. Creating Shared Value (Jan-Feb 2011 Issue), Harvard Business Review

92   In January 2007 The Body Shop and MTV announced a campaign to reach millions of under 25-year-olds around the world and launched a branded fragrance, the profits of which went to the Staying Alive Foundation.

93   Cray, Edward (1978) *Levi's: The "Shrink-to- Fit" business that stretched to cover the world*, Boston: Houghton Mifflin.

94   Tylenol was worth 17% of the company's net income at the time and the scandal caused it to plunge from 37% to 7% market share and almost destroyed the brand but the company CEO faced the issue head-on and "did the right thing" such that the brand was restored to prominence. Unfortunately for J&J there was another Tylenol for children recall in 2010, and the company was criticised by the FDA for being slow to correct manufacturing deficiencies.

95   Anderson, Ray and White, Robin (2009) *Confessions of a Radical Industrialist: How Interface proved that you can build a successful business without destroying the planet*, New York: Random House.

96   I worked with Golden Agri during this period and observed the review of its land holdings and the concessions made to conservation but no detailed information was ever made public of the costs to the company of its land set aside policies. The land held was an asset on the company's books and because of the lack of development it had no realisable value.

97   Watson, Thomas Jnr (1963) *A Business and its Beliefs*, New York: McGraw-Hill.

98   Chappell, Tom (1993) *The Soul of a Business: Managing for Profit and the Common Good*, New York: Bantam Books.

99   Anderson, Ray and White, Robin (2009) *Confessions of a Radical Industrialist: How Interface proved that you can build a successful business without destroying the planet*, New York: Random House.

100 Abrahams, Jeffrey (1995) *The Mission Statement Book: 301 Corporate Mission Statements from America's Top Companies*, Berkley, California: Ten Speed Press.

101 Friedman, Milton (1962) *Capitalism and Freedom*, Chicago: University of Chicago Press.

102 The Cadbury Ethical Trading and Human Rights Policy is available from the company.

103 The GRI began life in 1997 following the Exxon Valdez disaster in Alaska and the Coalition for Environmentally Responsible Economies with others began to press for better corporate reporting of economic, social and environmental performance. By 2016, it had developed into the Global Reporting Initiative based in the Netherlands and had launched the first ever global standard for sustainability reporting developed by a multi-stakeholder consultation process.

104 Clay, Jason (2005) Exploring the Links Between International Business and Poverty Reduction: A Case Study of Unilever Indonesia, Oxford: Oxfam and Unilever.

Chapter 8: The Management Challenge

105 Drucker, Peter (1985) *Innovation and Entrepreneurship*, London: Heinemann.

106 Grayson, David and Kakabadse, Andrew (February 2013) Sustainable Business Leadership – take it from the top, *Ethical Corporation Magazine*

107 The International Alliance for Responsible Drinking was launched in 2015 by 11 international drinks company CEOs. It is a non-profit organisation set up by the member companies and it has built on two decades of work by the International Center for Alcohol Policies and the Global Alcohol Producers Group and continues to reach out to a range of organisations in society around the world to address the issue of the misuse of alcohol.

108 The Dublin Principles were drafted in in 1997 after a multi-stakeholder consultation involving companies as a basis for future collaboration especially in respect of company funded research on alcohol problems.

109 IBM has a long and distinguished role as an innovator and contributor to the development of education first in the USA and then around the world. It has used a combination of its cash, equipment and software, with volunteers from the workforce and retirees, to help improve school-based education. Its Reinventing Education Initiative touched over 10 million students around the world and was independently assessed in 2001 to measure the positive contribution it was making to their performance.

110 King Taylor, Linda (2002) *Corporate Excellence in the Year 2000: Framework for Success*, London: Random House eBooks.

111 Browne, John, Nuttall, Robin and Stadlen, Tommy (2015) *Connect: How Companies Succeed by Engaging Radically With Society*, London: W.H. Allen.

112 Rosen, D., Chalkidou, K., and Madan Keller, J. (2017) An Initial Estimation of the Size of Health Commodity Markets in Low and Middle Income Countries, Washington: The Center for Global Development.

Chapter 9: Corporate Citizenship and the Future of Capitalism

113 Rothschild, Michael (1992) *Bionomics: The Inevitability of Capitalism*, London: Futura Publications.

114 Oxfam, (2017) *Reward Work Not Wealth*, Oxford: Oxfam.

115 Armitage, Jim (1st March 2017) Polman's proud record must not fall to slash and burn, *London Evening Standard*, Business Section.

116 Malnick, Edward (22nd November 2014) Food manufacturers 'should fund chewing gum clean-up costs', *Daily Telegraph*.

117 Narwan, Gurpreet (March 2nd 2018) Lego builds its future on plant-based plastic, *The Times* of London.

118 Harari, Yuval Noah (2011) *Sapiens: A Brief History of Humankind*, London: Penguin Random House.

119 Cray, Edward (1978) *Levi's: The "Shrink-to-fit" business that stretched to cover the world*, Boston: Houghton Mifflin.

120 Enron was the US energy company that went bankrupt in 2001 after using accounting loopholes and other means to distort its accounts and was the subject of a stockholder lawsuit. The CEO subsequently went to jail and the collapse of the company also led to the demise of its accounting firm Arthur Anderson.

121 Browne, John, Robin Nuttall and Tommy Stadlen (2015) *Connect: How Companies Succeed By Engaging Radically With Society*, London: W H Allen.

About the Author

David Logan is co-founder of Corporate Citizenship, the international consultancy widely regarded as a 'one-stop shop' for consulting on all aspects of corporate responsibility and sustainability. He has worked in the public, non-profit and private sectors and has 38 years of practical experience on frontline corporate responsibility and sustainability work.

In the 1970s, David worked as a teacher, then for the Trades Union Congress in London. As the Labour government of the day imploded, he left just before Mrs Thatcher was elected and worked for three years in the voluntary sector with unemployed young people. He worked with a successful, profit-making, community-owned business, one which was strongly supported by private companies. This experience encouraged him to 'switch sides' and in 1980 he joined Levi Strauss & Co. as manager of Community Affairs for Northern Europe.

He was later promoted to company headquarters in San Francisco, where he worked for the company's Ethics and Social Responsibility Committee on all aspects of corporate social responsibility. He dealt with issues as diverse as plant closures, HIV/AIDS, women's health provision, and purchasing from small minority firms. Since 1988, he has been a consultant on corporate social responsibility, and in 1996 was the co-founder of The Corporate Citizenship Company. It subsequently joined the Chime Group in 2007 and merged with The Smart Company to become Corporate Citizenship.

He has worked on corporate responsibility and sustainability issues in Europe, the USA and in over 30 developing countries and emerging markets of Africa, Asia and Latin America. He has also advised a wide range of international companies in industries as diverse as food and drinks, mobile phones, oil and pharmaceuticals, while working with clients such as Unilever, Cadbury and Abbott, for more than 10 years.

He is a graduate of London University, with a Masters in Philosophy and an Advanced Diploma in Education. He is an Associate Fellow at the Doughty Centre for Corporate Responsibility at Cranfield University in the UK.